Dreams from the Soul

TAYLAR PAIGE BROOKER

© Taylar Brooker, 2021

Disclaimer

The material in this publication is of the nature of general comment only and does not represent professional advice. It is not intended to provide specific guidance for any particular circumstances, and it should not be relied upon for any decision to take action or not to take action on any matter that it covers. To the maximum extent permitted by law, the author and publisher disclaim all responsibility and liability to any person, arising directly or indirectly from any person taking or not taking action based on the information in this book.

ISBN: pbk: 978-0-6453236-0-3

First published November 2021 by Taylar Brooker, www.MoonstoneGypsyAU.com

All rights reserved. Except as permitted under the *Australian Copyright Act 1968* (for example, fair dealing for the purposes of study, research, criticism or review), no part of this book may be reproduced, stored in a retrieval system, communicated or transmitted in any form or by any means without prior written permission. All inquiries should be made to the publisher.

Editing and design by Claire McGregor,
Kookaburra Hill Publishing Services

Illustrations: Cover: S. Hermann & F. Richter. Inside pages: StarGladeVintage; Gordon Johnson; Jo-B; Colleen ODell; Garik Barhegsyan; Open Clipart-Vectors; Prawny; Darkmoon Art; Carolina Ibarra-Mendoza; Tirriko; Venita Oberholster.

Dedication & Acknowledgement

I dedicate this book to all the free spirits, misfits, spiritualists, and beautiful souls who are finding their way in the world. May you find guidance and insight within the pages of this book and never stop believing in your dreams and the cosmic power they possess.

I owe a tremendous amount of gratitude to my beautiful family, friends, and spirit guides. Thank you for believing in me and encouraging me every step of the way.

To the hundreds of tarot clients I have read for over the years, I count my blessings that I have had the opportunity to connect with such amazing people.

*The dream is the small hidden door in the deepest
and most intimate sanctum of the soul, which opens
to that primeval cosmic night that was soul long before
there was conscious ego and will be soul far beyond
what a conscious ego could ever reach.*

~ CARL JUNG (1934)

Contents

Preface	1
Introduction to Dreams and Their Purpose	5
Dreams as teachers	11
Understanding consciousness	15
Which Category Do Your Dreams Belong To?	21
Clouded dreams	25
Ground-level manifestation dreams	30
Sparked dreams	33
Journey dreams	35
Natural Elements in Dreams	39
Earth, wind, fire, water	41
Wellbeing and Dreams	53
Emotions	55
Mindset	56
Spirituality	57
Physical body	58
Colours in Dreams	63
Colour dream example	65
Precognitive Dreams	69
Why do we have precognitive dreams?	71
Recurring Dreams	75
How to decipher your recurring dreams	78
Awakening Dreams	87
Universal dream symbols	91
Dreams of the Deceased	99

Dream Disorders — 105
Parasomnia — 107
Sleepwalking — 107
Night terrors — 108
Nightmares — 109
Violent and frightening dreams — 110

Spiritual Dream Attacks — 117
What are the triggers? — 120
Prevention — 123

Lucid Dreaming — 133
Have you experienced lucid dreaming? — 136
Downfalls of lucid dreaming — 137
Time to lucid dream! — 138

The Falling Sensation — 145
My understanding of the falling sensation — 148

Sleep Paralysis — 151
Do legends hold the answer to sleep paralysis? — 154
Mixed signals or spiritual experience? — 156

Astral Projection — 161
Question 1: What is the astral self/body? — 164
Question 2: What is the astral realm? — 166
Question 3: Why astral project? — 168
Question 4: Is astral projection safe? — 168
How to astral project — 169

Tools for Dream Work — 177
Four steps to remembering your dreams — 180

Dream Symbols and Metaphors — 201
Self-reflection — 204
Interpretation and understanding — 207

Your Journey — 225
About the Author — 226

Preface

The purpose of this book is to help you connect more deeply with your intuition, higher self, and dreams. By implementing the simple techniques and advice throughout each chapter about various types of dream work, you will find yourself developing your own ideas, approaches, and understanding of what your dreams are conveying to you. There is an abundance of personal potential and wisdom within every one of us, and dreams can open our eyes to powerful revelations, healing, life answers, and self-growth.

I wrote this book in honour of my Anaconda Spirit Guide, who first awakened my interest of the dream realm and the profound power it possesses. As my fascination with dreams deepened, I read countless books and articles that claimed to know what 'every' dream symbol meant. I was disheartened to notice a lack of creative, individual, philosophical, and spiritual views about dream symbols and metaphors.

Unfortunately, it is a frequent occurrence in our society to follow the crowd instead of expanding our mind with new knowledge, and allowing our intuition, personal beliefs, and dreaming experiences to guide us with the interpretation process. This is essentially what prompted me to take a risk and approach dream interpretation in a completely different direction to other people.

I was initially worried that I would be criticised or deemed 'wrong' with my openminded and spiritual views towards dreams. However, I believe you must trust and follow where your spirit guides, intuition, and passion lead you because if something is meaningful to you, then it will touch the hearts of others.

> *If we want to accurately explore and interpret our dreams, then we need to approach dream work with an open mind to every possible perspective.*

Below are several examples of the collectively shared views from numerous dream books, articles, and online forums:

* Dreams are a result of the subconscious mind processing information and nothing more.
* Dreams where people claim to experience visitations from religious/spiritual deities or deceased loved ones are generated solely from imagination and desire.
* Dreaming is not a spiritual or special experience; it is a psychological experience we are biologically programmed to do.
* Subconscious memories of people, places, and sex are the top dream themes.

Although I wholeheartedly agree and cannot deny that many of our dreams are the result of subconscious processing, I cannot help but feel a sense of restriction by this 'one answer fits all' to define every type of dream experience we have. If there is only one way to understand our dreams through the sole lens of the subconscious mind, then how can we possibly interpret dreams that have a spiritual, precognitive, past life, creative, or emotional element attached to them? The truthful answer is… we cannot. If we want to accurately explore and interpret our dreams, then we need to approach dream work with an open mind to every possible perspective.

Within this book, we will explore effective approaches on how to enhance your dream recall, categorise your dream experiences, and develop a deeper understanding of the symbolism, themes, and archetypes that appear in your dreams. By paying attention to the smallest details including the sounds, colours, situations, natural elements, energies, and environments that surface within your dream, you will gain a clearer understanding of who you are, what you are struggling with, what is holding you back, your strengths, and what steps you need to take to move forward in your life journey.

To enhance your dream, meditation, and astral projection experiences, you will be provided with a list of spiritual tools including crystals, herbs, oils, and dream journaling tips, which will assist in developing your psychic abilities. You will also find guidance on how to safely enter and return from the astral realm, raising your spiritual vibration from negative entities during an altered state of consciousness, simple steps to begin lucid dreaming, and discovering the meaning behind your recurring dreams and nightmares.

CHAPTER 1

Introduction to Dreams and Their Purpose

To dream is to essentially free oneself from earth-bound limitations, restrictions, and self-imposed bonds.

Introduction to Dreams and Their Purpose

Are dreams just figments of our imagination, or is there more to dreams than meets the eye? Dreaming is an incredibly personal, intuitive, and spiritual process that our psyche undergoes every time we fall asleep. While our physical body rests and our conscious mind shuts down momentarily from the stresses of life, our state of awareness shifts into the fantastical mode of dreaming. When we dream, our psyche follows a natural process of subconsciously channelling all the events that occurred within our day. Our psyche is the universal essence of our mind, soul, and spirit, and everything we experience throughout our lifetimes is stored within this part of us. Every emotion that was felt or repressed, every thought and idea conveyed in verbal conversation or withheld in the back of our mind, the situations, colours, smells, and personalities we encountered during our busy life schedule, are all processed through our altered state of consciousness when we dream.

It is only when we shift our state of awareness into a higher spiritual level – through dreaming and meditation – that we can properly access and open ourselves up to receiving the valuable lessons, insights, and worldly knowledge that we intentionally (and often unintentionally) learn from the relationships and interactions we have with other people, and from our own mistakes and triumphs. Ultimately, dreams are the gateway that allow us to connect with our collective consciousness, soul, and the spirit world.

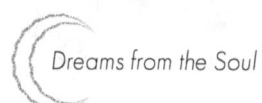
Dreams from the Soul

Dreams are a crucial component in our ability to learn, process, grow and evolve as we transcend through life's numerous obstacles, milestones, and experiences. As dreaming involves reaching an altered state of consciousness, this allows our higher self to freely traverse through the spiritual and universal realms, without being held back by worldly based inhibitions. During our time in the dream realm, we naturally heal our body both physically and spiritually, we restore balance to our chakras, and obtain answers, guidance, and solutions to the situations that plague us in waking life.

Take a moment to consider this question: Have you ever tried to remember the name of a song, place, or person and, despite your best efforts, you just cannot recall the answer?

Now, to everyone who answered 'yes', how many of you experienced a dream that suddenly prompted you to recall the answer you were looking for? Dreams provide symbolic clues to the questions we ask ourselves in waking life and relay insightful guidance using metaphors to help us subconsciously recognise what actions and decisions we must take to overcome dilemmas, indecisiveness, and confusion. When our conscious mind is pondering and cannot recall an answer or find a solution in waking life, often when we awaken from a restful night's sleep or abruptly jolt awake during our REM sleep cycle, the answer or solution to the conundrum we were trying to solve unexpectedly flows into our thoughts without any means of prompting. It is this type of scenario that provides proof to the powerful and meaningful function of our subconscious and unconscious mind in the dream realm, to access suppressed or forgotten information. This further reinforces the spiritual belief that our higher self truly does have the answers we are looking for.

Introduction to Dreams and Their Purpose

Dreaming allows us to escape the normality of our routine-based lives and venture into the universal planes, spirit realm, and our creative imagination, where we can embody and become the role of judge, jury, and executioner. In waking life, we are inadvertently and significantly influenced by materialism, cultural, societal, and religious expectations, the disheartening voice of our anxiety, insecurities, and peers, and the heavy burden of life's responsibilities. Yet during our time in the dream realm, we temporarily disconnect from these worldly aspects and stressors, and we gain the ability to objectively see our life and self for who we genuinely are, beyond what we are viewed as in the eyes of society.

Dreams play a phenomenal role in our personal growth and development.

We dream of desire, family, past lives, fear, anger, passion, fulfilment, memories, success, the future, fantasies, subpersonalities, memories, grief, violence, travel, death, and happiness… In other words, we dream about who we want to be, who we authentically are in our heart and soul, and what we want to experience during our lifetime. Dreaming allows us to safely diffuse and indulge built-up or repressed emotions, sexual tension, and creative ideas by providing us with a safe and private outlet for our fantasies, imagination, and shadow self. Discovering your true self and life's purpose through interpreting the symbolic messages in your dreams is an empowering path to pursue because dreams play a phenomenal role in our personal growth and development.

For those of you experiencing degradation and bullying in waking life, who are dealing with an existential crisis, are

struggling to find your identity and life's purpose, or feel disconnected from yourself and everyone around you, learning how to utilise the beautiful art of dream interpretation – and developing a deeper relationship with your higher self and spirit guides – will help you in your journey of healing and self-discovery.

A vast proportion of our dreams stem directly from the subconscious mind, where we intuitively project specifically chosen dream manifestations of archetypal characters, metaphors, environments, and themes. These manifestations include memories of workplaces, schools, homes, friends, family members, past lovers, and menacing animals or monsters, who represent those we dislike and feel overshadowed by in the physical world. When we dream of fighting off monsters, aggressive animals, or people, it is our mind's way of creating a safe outlet so we can subconsciously stand up, fight, and defeat the archetypal manifestations that portray similar domineering and hostile tendencies to those of our adversaries.

For those who struggle to walk away from controlling situations, or suffer from physical, emotional, and verbal abuse in everyday life, their dreams will possess an oppressive energy and often involve scenarios where they are being chased, belittled, humiliated, or physically bound. These negative dream themes reflect the individual's defeated mindset, psychological pain, and unwillingness or inability to remove themselves from their abusive life situation. However, when someone develops the strength to fight back and defend themselves in their dreams, it sparks a sense of courage in their subconscious mind. It serves as a powerful reminder to the individual that they do, in fact, have the power and inner strength to turn their life around. They have the potential to free themselves from the abuse, bullying, and control that others are inflicting upon them.

It is only in our dreams and imagination that we can completely control and express our reactions, thoughts, and responses without facing fear, ridicule, and judgement from others. It is an empowering experience to leave reality behind momentarily and travel through the dream realm, where we have freewill to do as we please, with nothing and no one to hold us back.

Dreams as teachers

The dreaming phenomenon has been discussed and debated significantly throughout history by scientists, accredited dream experts, philosophers, psychotherapists, spiritualists, and everyday people like you and me. Although we all have our own beliefs and understanding of what dreams represent and symbolise, whether they are derived from a religious, spiritual, or scientific belief system, there is one outstanding viewpoint we all share with one another: collectively, we agree that our dreams can have an undeniably significant impact on our mental health and self-esteem.

Despite the increase of interest and fascination towards dream interpretation in recent years, there are still those who strongly disagree with the Jungian philosophical theory that our dreams exist for meaningful or soul purposes. There are countless individuals who dispute the credibility and potential of dreams and deem them to serve no real valuable purpose in our lives. It is these obstinate statements, opposing opinions,

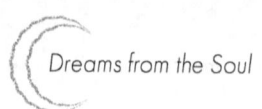

and lack of direction in the field of understanding and interpreting dreams that have consequently caused us to lose sight of the important fact that dreams are, and will always be, one of the most powerful teachers in our lifetime, if we allow them to be.

There is something deeper at work when we dream. Just because we cannot yet fully comprehend what dreams truly are, why we have them, and what influences us to dream such bizarre scenarios, does not mean we do not already have the underlying knowledge and ancient wisdom stored within our higher self to find out. We are all born with the ability to dream, and to have such an interesting ability and gift, we must question the special reason behind it. I believe everything living on Mother Earth, from human beings to all animals, dreams every time the sun sets and the moon shares her beautiful lunar energy with us. As a spiritualist, I view humans, animals, and nature as being interconnected on a spiritual and universal level.

Countless individuals conclude that they do not dream because they never remember their dreams upon waking, but I feel this statement is formulated through an insular mindset. If someone struggles to remember their dreams, I ask them whether they have ever tried dream journaling, meditation before bed, incorporating herbs, teas, and crystals to induce deeper dreaming experiences, or regularly practise mindfulness to help strengthen their ability to recall details from their dreams. Channelling and interpreting the messages from your dreams, and essentially just trying to remember your dreams is *not* something that will come naturally to everyone and will require patience and consistent effort on your part.

Introduction to Dreams and Their Purpose

Over the years, when discussing the topic of dream recollection with numerous people, I have found the individuals who are more spiritually awakened and in tune with their higher self and intuition have a much stronger ability to vividly recall their dream visions when compared to those who are more inclined to think logically and analytically in waking life.

We simply need to look through history at our native ancestors to see how connected they were to Mother Earth and all her creations, how they honoured Great Spirit through sacred ceremonies and ritual offerings, and how important they deemed dreams and visions to be. Looking back through historic petroglyphs and the legends of the dreamtime shared from various cultures and tribes all over the world, there is a clear link that early humankind deemed dreams as having an underlying spiritual, religious, and prophetic connection.

Dream journeying, interpretation, and storytelling were powerful and significant practices found among the Native American and Indigenous Australian cultures. It was during the dreamtime that the tribes' people were able to find and connect with their spirit power animal, receive warnings, obtain messages and guidance from Great Spirit, and experience visions of the past, present, and future. Traditionally, a tribe's shaman would enter an altered state of consciousness through meditation, ritual ceremony, or the dream realm, with the intention to ask the spirits for advice, knowledgeable teachings, and help regarding the issues the tribe's people were facing in waking life.

Our Indigenous ancestors used their dreams as a guideline when making important decisions for their tribe, especially when it came to matters of war, when to hold sacred

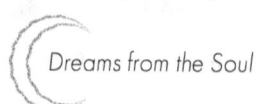
Dreams from the Soul

ceremonies for Great Spirit, where an adequate amount of food could be sourced, where to attack or hide from enemies, and relocating the tribe's location. During the time our ancestors walked freely among the land and lived off the Earth's natural resources, there of course was no access to the internet or dream-interpretation books. Yet not only could they recognise and understand the messages their dreams contained, but they also created artwork of their dreams and took part in storytelling ceremonies, where they recalled and recounted the various symbols, archetypes, messages, and spirits that appeared before them in the dream realm.

It is no wonder we cannot interpret our dreams because our minds are filled with so many distractions.

Fast-forward to living in today's fast-paced society and it is unquestionably clear how far we have drifted from the symbolic practices and spiritual belief systems of our ancestors. As we continue to evolve, we persistently distance ourselves from nature, spirit, intuition, and, consequently, the ability to recognise the true meanings of our dreams.

Our soul is a combination of spiritual essence, nature, life force, universal energy, and collective consciousness. It is these core elements that ultimately influenced and shaped the way our ancestors thought, interpreted dreams, and approached life. Because we now spend less time outdoors immersed in nature, often follow a strict routine and daily schedule, have an overwhelming amount of work, study, and responsibilities, fuel our bodies with fast food instead of proper nutrients, and fail to consistently practise adequate self-care and meditation, it is no wonder we cannot interpret our dreams because our minds are filled with so many distractions!

We have unintentionally learnt to block our clair-senses and overpower the voice of our intuition with ego, materialism, and through the constant stress and interferences occurring in our everyday life. Perhaps it is for this very reason that we have never lost our ability to dream, so that our spirit guides can communicate with us in such a way that ensures our higher self is open and receptive to the guidance, warnings, and knowledge being passed on to us.

Understanding consciousness

Before we immerse ourselves in the fascinating subject of dreams and the close connection dreaming shares with spirituality, it is important that you can differentiate and understand the various roles the consciousness undertakes, not just within the dream realm but also in everyday life. I have written a brief description of each level of consciousness, as I perceive it to be, from a spiritual and philosophical viewpoint. So, if at any time during this book you need to refresh your memory, you easily can.

I understand our mind's consciousness as a continuous natural cycle that processes similarly to the infinite Ouroboros. The Ouroboros symbolises the never-ending cycle of life, death, and rebirth. Through the depiction of a dragon (often interpreted as a snake) eating its own tail, the Ouroboros signifies the journey our soul undertakes through multiple lifetimes. During our time on Earth, while we are physically

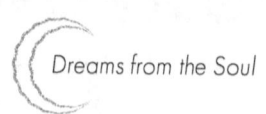

Dreams from the Soul

connected to everything and everyone around us, and up until the day we die and ascend into our spiritual body, our collective consciousness is the symbolic vessel for everything we feel, touch, think, hear, taste, see, memorise, and experience.

The mind is most often referred to as having three main levels of consciousness. We are going to explore each of these, and I have also included the concept of an altered state of consciousness (also known as state-change), as this occurs every time we drift to sleep, dream, meditate, intuitively write, undergo an out-of-body experience (OBE) or hypnosis, listen to music, and during mindful, relaxing, spiritual, or creative practices.

When we dream, our mind's consciousness naturally shifts into a dissimilar state of perception and awareness, which allows our psyche and right brain (associated with intuition, music, art, and creativity) to take over and influence our dream visions. It is during this state-change that we are intricately connected to our spiritual body, Crown Chakra (higher self/universal knowledge), Third Eye (pineal gland/spiritual eye), and are openly receptive to the intuitive messages from our spirit guides.

Each level of consciousness has a crucial role to play.

Conscious mind

Think of the conscious mind as the 'eye to the world'.

When you are awake, your mind's eye is constantly observing everything happening around you. This includes the sensations you feel, your instinctual reactions, and how you communicate and express yourself in situations.

Although the conscious mind can effectively and objectively make important decisions throughout your lifetime, this in turn must happen with the help of your subconscious mind. By drawing upon the information stored within the subconscious mind, you can consciously make a rational and calculative decision based upon past lessons, wisdom that has been passed on to you from mentors, and through the knowledge you have attained through life experience.

To effectively dream journey or meditate, we need to shift our conscious mind aside temporarily as it limits our capacity and ability to intuitively recognise and channel the energies, visions, and messages that are being projected through our subconscious mind and psyche. Our conscious mind is always observing and rationalising the events in our life, which is why we need to reach an altered state of consciousness to shift our conscious perspective aside. Our conscious mind often causes us to doubt, second guess, and downplay whenever we experience intuitive or spiritual phenomena.

Subconscious mind

Envision the subconscious mind as 'the ocean' as it is highly intriguing, forever flowing with information and memories, and it has the power to push and pull us in many directions.

Our subconscious runs deeper than our conscious mind as it absorbs and files away everything we have seen, felt, said, thought, and experienced during our life. No matter how much time passes between special occasions, significant life events, celebrations, sorrows, and traumas, certain details from these experiences are stored and filed away in our subconscious

mind. It is through dreaming, hypnosis, regression, daydreaming, shamanic practices, meditation, and psychotherapy that we can access and recall these memories from within our subconscious mind.

The subconscious mind acknowledges the patterns of our behaviour and thoughts. So, if you are someone who thinks negatively towards yourself, your subconscious mind will naturally become programmed to project pessimistic thought patterns. Therefore, it is vital when it comes to breaking cycles or bad habits that you adhere to strictly following a positive new behaviour or mentality. It takes several consistent weeks for the subconscious mind to process the new information and formulate a new thought pattern. Many of our dreams are manifested from the details our subconscious mind recalls; for example, life events, people, familiar environments, literature we have read, and movies we have watched.

Unconscious mind

The unconscious mind is the 'ultimate mystery' as it is completely invisible to the outside world. The unconscious is the window to our psyche, past lives, and universal knowledge and is the unfiltered reflection of who we are, at our core.

The unconscious mind is the deepest and truest connection we have to the spiritual realm, for it connects us with the lightness and darkness inside our soul. We are all capable of evil, and we are all capable of compassion, and our unconscious mind stores our deepest cravings, sexual urges, unfiltered emotions, and thoughts. These are often suppressed as we recognise we cannot act or behave towards others in such ways.

However, glimpses of our unconscious self can surface during certain situations; for example, having a heated argument with someone and unconsciously lashing out, either verbally or physically, instead of staying rational and calm as you consciously know you should.

When we say things like, "I don't know what came over me," "I don't know why I said that," "Where did that thought come from?" Or, "It was like I was a different person," these are glimpses into our unconscious self. During intense or overwhelming life situations, when we cannot control our urges or physical and emotional responses, we are momentarily confronted with a glimpse of our unconscious self that we normally would not show to the world (such as a subpersonality or repressed part of our nature).

Our unconscious is comparable to a Pandora's box as it withholds all our secrets, pain, fear, past-life memories, anxieties, unspoken ideas, primal instincts, desires, and details from our dreams. In Jungian terms, we might refer to the unconscious mind as being the shadow aspect of our personality. Our unconscious (shadow self) rarely makes an appearance in everyday life because we are too afraid to express our raw emotions, honest thoughts, and authenticity to ourselves and the world.

When presented with the opportunity to discover the shadow elements that exist within our psyche and unconscious, many people view this as a daunting task because it asks you to look deeper into yourself and question everything you claim to know, have been told, and believe in. Exploring your shadow self and unconscious mind will prompt you to acknowledge what you truly desire in the world, what you need to change, and what you are unhappy with. Turning within and connecting with your psyche for guidance and direction will help open your eyes to how strongly cultural, political, religious, and social influences impact your wellbeing, moral compass, universal values, mindset, and personal goals.

Altered state of consciousness

An altered state of consciousness (state-change) is when the conscious mind shifts into a higher state of intuitive awareness. Our connection to our higher self, spirit guides, and the universe becomes stronger when we shift our conscious mode of thinking.

Meditation, hypnotism, regression, dreaming, psychedelics, astral projecting, and spiritual practices are just a few examples of how we can alter our perception of physical reality and shift the mind's consciousness into a deeper and rhythmic pattern. The patterns of our brainwaves, heartbeat, and breathing begin to change (depending on what state-change method is being used, our heartbeat and breathing may increase and become erratic, or slow and relaxed), and our conscious mind remains aware of its surroundings, yet is no longer primarily focused on what is happening in the physical world or the concept of time for that matter.

Being in an altered state of consciousness helps the body to relax and release built-up emotions, tension, stress, anxiety, and overthinking.

CHAPTER 2

Which Category Do Your Dreams Belong To?

We never truly forget our dreams when spirit is involved. We hold on to the intuitive essence and spiritual wisdom that is shared with us, within our soul and consciousness.

Which Category Do Your Dreams Belong To?

It is human nature to automatically categorise and judge one another based on age, gender, physical appearance, culture, religion, social status, and material wealth. Within one moment of meeting someone, we instantly decide what type of person they are, how to communicate and respond to them, and ultimately whether we like their energy and persona. It is through our intuition and instincts that we unconsciously recognise negative and positive energy, potential threats and deception, and characteristic traits we like and dislike in others.

When we over-analyse our dreams and read too deeply into something that is not there, we can easily lose sight of what is clearly in front of us.

Before we attempt to understand and interpret our dreams, or the dreams of others, we need to focus less on trying to make logical sense of the dreaming experience and be mindful not to rationalise every detail we can recall. When we over-analyse our dreams and read too deeply into something that is not there, we can easily lose sight of what is clearly in front of us. When looking at dreams, one of the first things we need to take into consideration is what 'category' the dreaming experience falls under. Just as we categorise places, people, styles, and situations in waking life, we should do so with

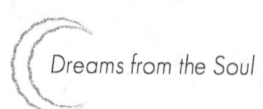

our dream visions because it makes interpreting them much easier. When we know what type of dream we are dealing with, only then can we appropriately decipher and respond to it accordingly.

Over the years, after interpreting my own dream experiences and the dream accounts others have shared with me, I have developed a unique system for effectively understanding, categorising, and interpreting the symbolic and metaphorical messages our dreams are conveying to us. It is a simple yet explorative system that allows you to more easily pinpoint where your dream has come from, what it is trying to convey to you, and why such a dream may have arisen in the first place.

To begin, let us explore the four categories dreams can be divided into:

1) Clouded dreams
2) Ground-level manifestation dreams
3) Sparked dreams
4) Journey dreams

Although the majority of the time you can easily pinpoint which category your dreaming experience belongs to, you should not limit yourself by trying to interpret a dream's meaning based solely on the category alone. Everything written in this book should be used as a guide to help steer you in the right direction with your dream interpretation, but never replace what your intuition and higher self are telling you. By working with your intuition and a dream system you believe in, you will find yourself learning about not only your dreams but also the remarkable way your psyche and spirit guides communicate with you, through carefully chosen symbols, metaphors, archetypes, and dream synchronicity.

Let us explore each dream category and see where your dream experiences belong.

Clouded dreams

Dark, disturbing, and violent dreams. Nightmares and night terrors fall into this category.

Dreaming experience

The themes of helplessness, pain, violence, and fear that are featured in clouded dreams will cause the dreamer to feel unrested, negative-minded, irritable, and emotional for the day ahead. This is due to the combination of adrenaline, stress, fear, and the disturbing dream themes that remain present in the dreamer's mind.

In waking life

Clouded dreams are most frequently triggered by emotional and mental imbalance, lack of safety and security, and when the physical body is pushed beyond its window of tolerance. Triggers include:

- recalling traumatic memories
- high stress levels and body burnout
- abuse of all kinds
- emotional pain and turmoil (e.g., the sudden death of a loved one, divorce, diagnosis of a terminal illness)

- strong feelings of resentment, anger, sadism, and violence
- substance abuse and addiction
- mental health conditions where the mind, emotions, and spirit are disconnected and unstable (e.g., depression, anxiety, schizophrenia, bipolar disorder, PTSD).

Common clouded dream symbols can include:

- violence (the dreamer may be experiencing or inflicting pain onto others)
- dark and gloomy colours
- storms
- sparse scenery (lack of vibrancy and details)
- mutilation and torture
- weapons
- humiliation (the dreamer may be laughed at, embarrassed, or wearing inappropriate clothing or no clothing at all)
- running away and trying to escape from someone/something
- being lost in a maze
- monsters and disfigured dream characters
- psychic and spiritual attacks.

Clouded dream interpretation

The following clouded dream was shared by a lovely woman who was seeking clarification about the meaning of her dream. She suffered from anxiety, but recently her panic attacks were happening more frequently, due to her workplace colleagues bullying her.

A tall man with black eyes is stalking me through the streets. As I begin to run, he follows behind and I know he's going to hurt me. As I'm trying to run faster, I see a green car approaching in the distance, and I manage to jump inside the passenger seat. The car continues to drive and drops me off beside a large lake of water, and I'm suddenly really relaxed.

A breakdown of the dream symbols would be as follows:

* The 'tall man' is symbolic of the work colleagues who bully and negatively impact the dreamer's mental health.
* The 'stalking and harmful threat' of the tall man reflects how the dreamer feels victimised and targeted at work.
* The 'car' as a dream symbol stands for movement, travel, and direction.
* The emphasis of the car being the colour 'green' represents freedom and space.
* The 'large lake' symbolises possibility, peacefulness, and emotional contentment.

The dreamer is unconsciously guiding herself to realise that she needs to break away from her current workplace (the tall man), for the sake of her wellbeing and emotional health. She needs to make the conscious decision to move forward with her life because there are other career opportunities available around her (green car arriving). She needs to be willing to step out of her comfort zone (green car driving to an unknown destination with her in the passenger seat) and apply for a position at a new workplace (being dropped off next to the lake), as she will find contentment in a new workplace environment (relaxed feeling).

Clouded dreams and the Spirit World

Clouded dreams also have a direct connection to psychic and spiritual attacks. When someone is suffering, grieving, or experiencing significant hardship in their life, their spiritual vibration (auric energy) is lowered, which can potentially cause them to become more receptive to spiritual attacks, psychic vampires, and negative entities. This is when spiritual beings who carry emotional debris, turmoil energies, and negative intentions will surface in the dream realm and manifest in the forms of darkness, shadows, and disturbing and frightening dream themes.

The solution

If you or anyone you know falls into the category of clouded dreaming, please consider integrating the following advice into everyday life:

* *Pay close attention.* Be honest with yourself and reflect on the potential triggers in your life that may be causing such negative dream visions to arise. For example, the trigger could be you, other people, an environment, situation, or impending future event that is weighing your mind down. You may also not be acknowledging, accepting, or dealing with an important problem/situation in your life, which requires immediate follow-through for the sake of your health, security, safety, or future.
* *Clear your mind through deep breathing, mindfulness, or meditation.* Before you go to bed each day, dedicate several minutes (without any kind of distraction) to reflect on all the events that surfaced during your day.

You should not try to control what flows through your mind, or stop any unexpected memories, questions, or thoughts that seem to arise of their own accord (as these are the aspects your subconscious mind wants to bring to your attention momentarily). After a few minutes, your mind will begin to quieten and become uncluttered, which will help your body enter a parasympathetic state. This simple step of properly relaxing and unwinding the body and mind before you drift to sleep will help induce peaceful and positive dreams.

* *Raise your spiritual (auric) vibration.* It is essential that anyone who experiences regular clouded dreams, night terrors, sleep paralysis, nightmares, or spiritual/psychic attacks develops a deeper relationship with their spirit guides and grounds themselves regularly in nature.

  Raising your vibration is when you strengthen your connection to your mind, body, and spirit to create a deeper state of harmony and positivity within yourself. This can be achieved through regularly practising mindfulness, meditation, and earthing. These practices help to clear negative thought patterns, unblock your Crown and Root chakras, and connect you with positive white light energy.

  Reiki or crystal healing can help restore a positive flow of energy within your chakras by removing stagnant, lingering, or toxic energies from the negative people (psychic vampires) and environments you have encountered. Shamanic healing can be used to sever or heal negative attachments from past lives or spiritual entities and restore any disharmony that may exist within your spirit, soul, or mind. The practice of prayer will help you connect more deeply with your spirit guides and angels for protection, guidance, and healing.

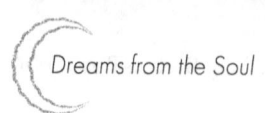
Dreams from the Soul

Note: you do not need to follow every approach I have listed. Simply find a practice that works well for you and is something you can commit to doing.

Ground-level manifestation dreams

Dreams involving celebrities, school, work, public transport, exams, and people you know.

Ground-level manifestation dreams are built upon the combination of desire, relationships, social interaction, and the media. They are inspired by external distractions and subconscious thoughts and memories.

Dreaming experience

Ground-level manifestation dreams have a direct link to the conversations, routines, and familiar environments and people that the dreamer encounters during their life journey. This dream category connects most strongly with our subconscious mind, attitude, ambition, desires, and everything we are influenced by in waking life, including our peers and social media. In ground-level manifestation dreams the dreamer will subconsciously project certain themes from life events, personal experiences, and underlying fantasies into their dream visions. This is often done to indulge a desire, or to change (recreate) an entirely new outcome for a situation they experienced in the past, so it is more fulfilling, satisfying, and positive for their ego.

For example, I would like you to reflect on a situation from your past that did not turn out the way you initially hoped it would. Perhaps you got into a fight with your boss and did not say what you really wanted to at the time, and it keeps hovering in your mind as a regret. In a ground-level manifestation dream, this is where your subconscious mind and imagination will re-enact/recreate this experience and change the outcome, so you can finally say what you initially held back from your boss.

Ground-level manifestation dream example

The following example was passed on to me from a stranger, who wanted an outsider to interpret her dream objectively and intuitively. The dreamer is in her mid-twenties and lives with three housemates, who are always at home. She is studying at university, working part-time, and trying to juggle several other personal commitments but is struggling to cope.

> *I'm sitting in a field with millions of colourful and blooming flowers all around me. I cannot see my face, but I know I'm smiling. As I'm sitting down looking around me, I can hear the ticking of a clock and it starts raining heavily, drowning all the flowers into the ground. I am left sitting in mud while the clock keeps ticking.*

A breakdown of the dream symbols would be as follows:

✷ 'Sitting down' represents that the dreamer needs to take a break and rest her body.

(Note: what your dream self is doing with your body in dream scenarios can often provide insight to the state of your wellbeing and energy levels.)

✷ 'Colourful blooming flowers' represents happiness, uplifted mindset, and peace.

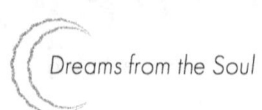

- The 'field' relates to tranquillity and personal space, especially because no other dream characters are present.
- The sound of the 'ticking clock' is symbolic of deadlines, schedules, rushing, and awaiting an impending outcome.
- Rainfall that 'drowns' the flowers into the ground reveals the dreamer's peace of mind is being interrupted by outside influences and responsibilities.

Interpretation

The dreamer is not giving herself a chance to sit down, relax, or ground in a natural environment (sitting in a field of flowers with no one around) where paperwork, time, and other people cannot distract her. Because she constantly runs her life by a strict time schedule, it is beginning to have an increasingly draining effect on her creative imagination, mindset, and spirit (the downpour of rain that leaves her sitting in mud). Consequently, unless the dreamer can create more balance and personal downtime in her life, the ticking clock is an impending warning that she will physically and mentally drain herself to the point where she has no choice but to stop.

Are your dreams intriguing or mundane?

Ground-level manifestation dreams tend to be both an imaginative and direct reflection of our life, attitude, and interests. Since this category of dreams is triggered by our own personality and perspective on life, this can mean our dreams could be incredibly uplifting, colourful, and adventurous, or they could be considerably uneventful and mundane. The theme of ground-level manifestation dreams depends on who we are as individuals and how we perceive and approach the world around us.

For example, those who surround and immerse themselves in nature, art, positive relationships, and books will have an incredibly different dreaming experience compared to those who spend the majority of their time glued to social media and obsessing over the lives of celebrities and superficial façades.

Sparked dreams

New ideas, creativity, answers, and solutions.

Sparked dreams are prompted by intuitive thoughts, subconscious and unconscious suggestions and creative ideas. To experience a sparked dream denotes that new beginnings, interests and personal potential are ready to be discovered.

Dreaming experience

Trying to recall answers, seeking solutions to problems, learning new skills and talents, decision-making, creative thinking, future planning, and tapping into undiscovered potential and talents all fall into the category of sparked dreams. This type of dreaming manifests insightful, intuitive, forward thinking, and inventive ideas, and provides guidance to those seeking clarification, confidence, and direction in waking life. The psyche has the perfect opportunity to 'spark' when it enters an altered state of consciousness for dreaming as it allows our higher self to unbiasedly comprehend life situations, reflect on choices that need to be made, discover unacknowledged gifts and abilities, and problem-solve obstacles with greater clarity and unhindered intuitive guidance.

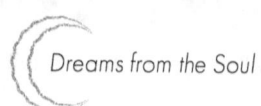

Common sparked dream symbols include:

* pregnancy and giving birth
* discovering a key, present, or door
* rainbows
* shooting stars
* receiving a letter
* element of fire
* sparklers
* birds (Spirit Bird is an animal messenger who delivers news and fresh perspectives).

Sparked dream scenario

If you are ever uncertain about a decision you need to make, have unanswered questions, feel lost and without a direction, or need to get your creativity flowing again, then learning how to induce and work with sparked dreams will help you immensely and boost your self-confidence.

Sparked dreams occur more frequently than you may think and help to influence the way you formulate business plans, confront obstacles and relationship issues, how you overcome challenges and learn from your mistakes, and ultimately when you feel the unexpected urge to make a drastic life change or pursue a new path.

Before you try to induce a sparked dreaming experience, ensure you do so with an open heart and mind. Quite often, the messages, ideas, and answers that flow through from our higher self are not necessarily what we would have considered when thinking with our rational and calculative mind.

However, this is the beauty of sparked dreams as they prompt you to think bigger about yourself and your life, what you are capable of doing and what options are available to you.

If you are seeking guidance about something, looking for answers, or want something more from your life, then before you drift to sleep at night program the intention firmly in your mind: *I am ready to receive insight and revelations from my dreams.* Ensure you are writing down your dreams whenever you recall them because your answer will come to you in a repeated dream metaphor, theme, synchronistic sign, or intuitive thought. Be patient and openminded to what your higher self communicates to you in sparked dreams... it may well change the course of your life and help you discover your soul's purpose.

Journey dreams

Connection to your higher self and the spirit world.

Journey dreams are a spiritual and prophetic experience. When you enter an altered state of consciousness through spiritual outlets, meditation, and dreaming, your psychic abilities and intuition become stronger and more receptive to the energies and messages from spirit.

The history of journey dreams

The stories and legends of dreamtime journeying relate back to our ancestors. Every culture – although divided by spiritual and religious deities, tribal rituals, and universal values – ultimately share the similar belief that 'human and spirit are one in the dream plane'. When we dream, we enter a reality that bypasses

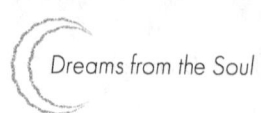

the rules and physics of our everyday reality. There is no concept of time, or interruption from self-biased, egotistical, and disheartening thoughts, which normally override the voice of our higher self and ability to connect with the spirit world.

Throughout history, there has been a staggering number of stories shared by people who claim to have experienced flashbacks of their past lives, glimpsed into the future, or have been visited by angels, deceased loved ones, and spiritual beings while dreaming. Journey dreams will often be experienced when the dreamer needs healing of some kind, during a spiritual awakening, seeking reassurance and guidance in waking life, during times of grief and loss, and when a message or warning needs to be received.

Just because you cannot consciously recall experiencing a journey dream, does not mean you have not been visited by your spirit guides, or received intuitive insight that has later helped you in life. An individual's spiritual beliefs and attitude towards themselves and the world will determine how their spirit guides choose to communicate with them. Due to many people being closed-off from their spiritual nature and intuition, spirit guides will often project repetitive symbols (words, numbers, themes, objects, etc.) into the dream realm. Although consciously the message may not be recognised by the dreamer, the guidance will be stored in the dreamer's psyche, where it will later flow through their thoughts unexpectedly.

Common journey dream symbols include:

* presence of spiritual deities (spiritual beings and passed loved ones will often communicate with you verbally or telepathically in a journey dream)
* rising kundalini energy

- ✷ the arrival of your spirit animal
- ✷ a disembodied voice that offers guidance, answers, or revelations (this can be your higher self or spiritual beings)
- ✷ appearing back in time during a different era
- ✷ wandering in a desert or being submerged in a large body of water (these symbols are highly spiritual and powerful omens that represent rebirth, transformation, and awakening).

It is important to mention that journey dreams are unique for every individual and cannot be interpreted by relying solely on symbols and themes alone. The energy, emotions, and responses that surface from your dream experience will instantly confirm that the dream was indeed 'special' and undeniably significant for you. Often, journey dreams can appear when you are contemplating a big life change, refusing or failing to acknowledge your true potential and abilities, when endings and new beginnings are ready to take place, or simply when your spirit guides recognise that you are ready to receive insight and messages.

Journey dream interpretation

Just before I embarked on my tarot-reading journey and had only been recording my dreams for a few months, I had a powerful journey dream that involved my spirit animal and rising kundalini energy. For reference, 'kundalini rising' signifies the rising or awakening of metaphysical and universal energy from within your mind, body, and spirit. Everyone interprets and describes kundalini differently but, in my eyes, it represents our higher self becoming more in-tune and aware of spiritual energy, new perspectives, creativity, universal knowledge, motivation, and inspiration. The kundalini is often depicted as a snake rising or uncoiling from the base of the spine (Root Chakra), rising upwards through our chakras, and reaching the top of our head (Crown Chakra), where a deeper state of self-awareness, intuition, clearer dreams and meditative visions, or sudden realisation of what our soul's purpose or next path will be.

> *I am walking down a road with my nan, and we are passing houses and making our way to a forest that lies ahead of us. As we turn to pass the forest, a large anaconda (which is also my spirit animal) slithers alongside me on the road and makes its way to the forest. My nan is scared and says it will hurt us and starts to walk in a different direction, but I assure her the snake means no harm. My nan suddenly disappears from the dream, and I have turned around to look up at a large oak tree in the middle of the forest. I see the anaconda wrapping itself around the trunk of the tree. I stand and watch the anaconda (she had a distinct female energy) as she coiled around the tree and travelled towards the top. I was fascinated and relaxed as I watched the process, and eventually turned to walk away just before the dream ended.*

Before this dream took place, I had no prior knowledge about what kundalini was, nor what it represented! The moment I awoke from the dream and recorded it in my journal, I instantly knew it was important and symbolised spiritual energy and personal growth. This journey dream opened my eyes to spirituality and dreams in a more profound way, and I feel it helped to lead me in the direction of tarot reading and meditation.

CHAPTER 3

Natural Elements in Dreams

There is no separation between the natural elements and human beings. We channel fire when we are overcome with rage and passion; water appears in our tears and heartfelt emotions; air is the constant chatter of our thoughts; and earth is how we care for our physical wellbeing.

Earth, wind, fire, water

The four elements symbolise the metaphysical, physical, and spiritual attributes of our beautiful universe and all living creatures. Everything in nature has its order, purpose, and ability to combine and create a powerful ecosystem that allows for the natural transition of death, life, and rebirth to occur.

Every universal element possesses its own unique symbology and underlying cosmic energy. What sets the four elements apart, when compared to other dream symbols, is the distinct and powerful connection the elements have to our primal and spiritual nature. No matter what context the natural elements appear within our dreams, whether it is believed to be a positive or negative manifestation from our subconscious mind, the elements will always offer ancient and universal teachings to those who are willing to listen. We as humans and spiritual beings are closely intertwined with the workings of nature. Just as our native ancestors learned to predict, channel, and work with the natural elements, we too can utilise and work with the energy of the elements in our dreams.

The more closely you pay attention and become consciously aware of the natural elements, weather, and scenery that appear in your dreams, not only will your intuitive and interpretative ability become stronger, but you also take one step closer to mastering the art of lucid dreaming, which we will discuss later.

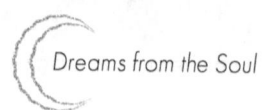
Dreams from the Soul

Although the natural elements that appear in the dream realm will often be a result of the dreamer's attitude, emotions, thought patterns, or life situations, they can also be manifested from a higher spiritual power and align with the changing of seasons. When universal and planetary shifts are occurring within the dreamer's life, and throughout the world, the natural elements will repeatedly surface in dream visions to gain our undivided attention.

Let us explore the natural elements as dream symbols.

Spirit of fire

Rebirth, transformation, and personal power.

Spirit of fire embodies the powerful energy of transition, change, lust, evolution, death, creativity, passion, and personal potential. When fire appears in the dream realm, you need to remain open and receptive to the powerful changes that will manifest in its wake. Spirit of fire has symbolically shifted the stagnant energy from your life, with the intention for you to begin a new path. There is nothing standing in your way now as fire has burned away all the limitations and doubts from your mind and calls forth your confidence and ambition to help guide you on your next journey.

Fire is a destructive yet purifying force that helps break down the strong insecurities, self-loathing, emotional pain, obstacles and hesitations that prevent you from moving forward.

Personal connection

Fire resonates with the building of emotions, temper, energy, words, actions, and physical situations. Just as fire takes time to completely burn out of control, we too must be able to recognise the signs within ourselves when we are about to reach our breaking point and unleash an intense outpouring of suppressed tension, deep-rooted emotions, frustration, and unbalanced energy.

For those who have a short temper, anger easily, lash out abruptly and are often hot-headed when dealing with others, seeing the presence of fire in the dream realm symbolises the uncertain yet impending impact your hostile behaviour will cause in the future. Fire often appears when a warning, wake-up call, or shift in attitude needs to take place, and when impending life changes are on their way and need to be embraced.

When the element of fire is projected into dreams it will not always appear as 'fire' itself but instead in the form of a symbolic metaphor. In the dream realm if you were to see flames, smoke, firecrackers, meteorites, volcanos, acting/drama classes, explosions, fighting, sex, warzones, work promotions, or a sudden revelation/breakthrough, then these can all represent the energy of fire.

Below are several reasons why fire most often appears in the dream realm. However, there is no one answer that fits all, and the natural elements may have a completely different reason for visiting you in your dreams!

Fire dream meanings:

※ Sparked imagination, creative thinking, and a sudden realisation of what is profoundly important to you.

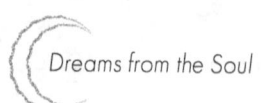
Dreams from the Soul

- Discard illusions and disillusions you have unintentionally created or become accustomed to living with.
- Speak openly and honestly about how you feel and what you think to obtain liberation and freedom.
- Find self-confidence in yourself once again.
- Release built-up emotions and thoughts in a safe way (letting go of unnecessary anger, frustration, and hate).
- Make a beneficial change sooner rather than later, so consider what aspect within your life or self needs to adapt and transform.
- Reflect on your current path, mentality, decisions, and behaviour as all actions have consequences.
- Make time for passion, love, romance, and sensuality.

Spirit of water

Healing, personal growth, and introspection.

Spirit of water symbolises the depths of your unconscious mind; a place where emotions, matters of the heart, and unspoken words remain hidden. Spirit of water is perhaps the most inspiring and nurturing element of them all.

When water appears before you in the dream realm, know that you are ultimately being guided and healed by the universe. Your troubled thoughts, unbalanced energy, and any dis-ease present within your wellbeing is slowly restoring itself. Just like the natural flowing movement of water, you will experience waves of emotion and bouts of uncertainty as life opens and closes doors of opportunity, invokes lessons, and invites new experiences. It is during these transitional times, when everything is changing around you, that spirit of water wants you to understand and trust the process, even when you feel lost.

Spirit of water channels the unfathomable depths of the unconscious mind and helps you undergo a profound sense of emotional release and spiritual growth.

Personal connection

Water has a natural connection to empaths and those who have depression, anxiety, and mental illness. I have heard stories of people who suffer with depression and seek the help of a shaman or spiritual healer to help alleviate the pain and suffering in their psyche. The depressed individuals are led either in 'meditative vision or in real life' to a body of water, where they will be momentarily submerged, and the heavy thoughts, unbalanced emotions, and past traumas will be released. When they arise from the water and return to shore, they have released all the pain from within their soul. The element of water cleanses and purifies the spirit and soul, which provides an individual who never had purpose, happiness, or peace before in their life with the opportunity to finally see their life and self with a clear, unburdened, and hopeful perspective.

When water appears before you in the dream realm it reflects what is happening within your metaphysical body. How the energy of water is projected into your dreams (the symbology in which it appears) is key to understanding

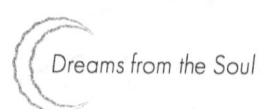

whether you are on the cusp of developing a deeper relationship with your authentic self and finding your place in the world, or whether it appears in a negative context that mirrors your feelings of loneliness, disconnection, and unsatisfaction.

Unlike the other natural elements, the element of water is easy to recognise in dreams as it always appears specifically in the form of water. For example, oceans, rivers, waterfalls, tears, drowning, rain, storms, pools, tsunamis, and rainforests. Water may also manifest itself using various shades of blue and green, so take note of whether these colours are continually appearing in your dreams.

Water dream meanings:

- Encourage free-flowing thoughts and introspection.
- Discover newfound beliefs and spiritual gifts.
- Accept yourself and what you consider to be your faults.
- Understand that your life is forever moving, and nothing lasts forever (learning how to adapt to change rather than fighting against it).
- Realise the importance of letting go and not holding on to people, places, emotions, habits, behaviours, or negative thought patterns that hinder your ability to grow positively as a person.
- Open yourself up to the spirit world and universe.
- Listen to the voice of your intuition rather than doubting and ignoring it.
- Release emotions and pain.
- Keep your mind and heart open to synchronistic signs.

> *As a spiritualist, I believe spirit of water is the most powerful element to cleanse and release negativity, burden, pain, heartbreak, self-destructive habits, and grief.*

Spirit of air

As the wind changes direction, so does your destiny.

Spirit of air is a beautiful element that carries the energy of possibility, good luck, taking chances and calculated risks. As the wind blows and crosses your life path, the arrival of news, ideas, and opportunities will soon appear before you.

When the element of air appears in the dream realm, it is a clear and concise message that you need to step back momentarily from the hustle and bustle of life, objectively look at any problems or situations you need to deal with, and remember to breathe deeply. It is only when you allow yourself the freedom to stand still and be present that you truly gain a higher perception of where you currently are, what you are struggling with, and what you are working towards.

Spirit of air understands the importance of having guidance in your life and asks you to turn within to your higher self for this wisdom. Just as wind has travelled the world, you too have crossed paths with millions of people, both in this lifetime and your previous lives, and the knowledge you have unconsciously absorbed from these experiences can guide you on many levels.

Dreams from the Soul

Personal connection

The element of air wants you to appreciate the process of 'inner growth' that occurs within you as you learn to rise above and overcome troubling and turbulent times. You cannot control or try to tame the way in which the wind blows, just as you cannot maintain a constant state of equilibrium within yourself or life. Allow everything – passing emotions, thoughts, fears, doubts, relationships, and situations – to drift from your life naturally as the universe has intended them to. Wind serves as a constant reminder to never look back at what you regret, but rather look forward because change and new beginnings are only a breath of wind away.

Air will appear in the dream realm using metaphorical symbols, such as cyclones, tornados, wind, puzzles, crossroads, arrows, whispering, and clouds. When the element of air is projected into your dreams, consider where your time, focus, and energy have been directed for the past several weeks.

Air dream meanings:

* Clear the mind of scattered and unhelpful thoughts.
* Re-establish your priorities.
* Approach matters of life with objectivity and intuition (do not be afraid to shift your perspective and trust your instincts).
* Make time for meditation and self-reflection (the element of air resonates with intuitive thoughts and the collective consciousness).
* The importance of timing is crucial, and nothing will happen before it is meant to (do not become impatient or disheartened when things do not unfold as you originally expected them to).

* Contemplate what steps you are going to take next in life. (What are you working towards?)
* Ask yourself what you are holding on to from your past and say it aloud as the wind blows (the element of wind will carry away your troubles and worries).

It is through the passing wind that Great Spirit whispers her wisdom and encouragement to those feeling restricted and aspiring to find the path that is meant for them.

Spirit of earth

Channel Mother Earth's abundant lifeforce and grounding energy.

Spirit of earth has a deep and profound attachment to our physical health and the way in which we judge ourselves and others. For us to reach our highest potential and achieve our life goals, we must be willing to dedicate a tremendous amount of effort, time, and attention to them without becoming distracted or neglectful along the way. Spirit of earth recognises that to create stability, strong foundations, and good health requires commitment and patience to bring these elements into fruition.

When the energy of earth is projected into the dream realm, it is a reminder to the subconscious mind and ego that material-related matters and following strict routines should not always be the centre of your attention. Spirit of earth understands the importance of building a prosperous and successful life, but that spending adequate time with loved

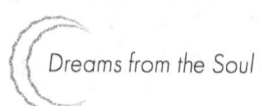

ones and outside in nature needs to be regularly integrated into your weekly routine. This simple practice will help you remain humble and grounded during every stage in your life journey.

Personal connection

When the element of earth makes an appearance in your dreams, it is because you need a gentle reminder to ground your mind, body, and soul. To establish a deeper sense of balance, tranquillity, and acceptance within yourself, you must reconnect with nature because it holds the universal energy of strength, healing, power, and knowledge.

If you relate to any of the following statements below, please follow spirit earth's guidance and begin regularly spending more time in nature. It will help clear the objectivity that has clouded your mind and outlook on life.

- *I become caught up in focusing on other people's lives and compare them to my own.*
- *I feel like I'm lacking in some type of way and think negatively about myself and what I have achieved so far in my journey.*
- *I only acknowledge my mistakes and don't give myself enough credit for my successes.*
- *I judge others and determine their worth based on their financial status and career position.*
- *I am driven by money, power, and fame (recognition) rather than having a genuine passion for what I do.*
- *I constantly feel drained, unhopeful, and in a negative mindset.*

Earth in the dream realm demonstrates the importance of spending time outdoors with natural light, air, sounds, and smells. The effortless tasks of walking outside barefoot, swimming in the ocean, hugging a tree, going for a hike, watching birds fly through the sky, and feeling the warmth of the sun on your skin is how the element of earth wants you to channel the relaxing and grounding energy of Mother Nature.

The element of earth will use an array of symbols in dreams, including sand, soil, rocks, plants, herbs, fields, trees, flowers, picnics, paddocks, valleys, and mountains.

Earth dream meanings:

- Disconnect from social media and do something productive with your time.
- Find a healthy balance between home and work life.
- Do not let yourself feel guilty for needing to take a break, changing priorities, and asking others for help.
- Stop telling yourself you should be doing more or feeling that you do not measure up to societal expectations.
- Reflect on your blessings and be grateful for everything you have in the present moment. Happiness must be found in what you have, rather than relying on what may arrive in the future.
- Dedicate more time to being outdoors in nature and moving your body.

Disconnect from the busyness of life to reconnect with the earth's unconditional love, healing, and ancient knowledge.

CHAPTER 4

Wellbeing and Dreams

Dreaming is a glimpse into the soul, the worlds in between, and the love within our being.

We are composed of mind, body, spirit, emotion, and energy. Dream interpretation is predominantly approached through the sole lens of subconscious mind processing. However, this approach consequently leads us to forget that our body, emotions, and spiritual nature can also influence our dreams. When we are experiencing high-stress situations, trying to cope with physical ailments, battling our inner demons, expressing an unhealthy ego, exploring our psychic gifts and during times of emotional distress, our dreams will channel the energy from these parts of ourselves. Expand beyond the 'subconscious mind' with your approach to dream work and look at your dreams from every lens of your wellbeing.

Emotions

Our emotions play a significant part in shaping the way our dreams portray messages of healing, support, and guidance to us. When our emotions enter a state of overwhelming distress, anxiety, or a period of depression, it profoundly impacts our thought patterns, outlook, self-esteem, and motivation levels – all of which inadvertently projects melancholy and turmoil energy into our dreaming experiences.

Dream symbols associated with emotions include:

* the element of water
* the moon, night sky, and stars

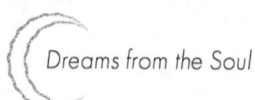

- clouds
- loss/losing something
- thunderstorms
- forests
- objects that reflect your appearance (e.g., mirrors, windows, reflective pools of water)
- crying/tears
- Heart and Throat chakras
- flowers (especially lilies and lotus flowers)
- chest pain (this dream symbol often surfaces when heartbreak or the loss of something meaningful is occurring in waking life).

Mindset

(Inflated ego/negative attitude)

Those who are driven by their ego, pessimism, a judgemental attitude, superficial façades, and materialism in waking life, generally dream of 'being in control or fighting'. They will often dream of dominating other dream characters with their words, power, or fists. Individuals who are competitive and driven by the need to do better than others will often experience unimaginative and stereotypical dream scenarios.

Dream symbols associated with an inflated ego/negative attitude include:

- obstacle courses and rollercoasters
- competitions (often cheating to win or sabotaging other dream characters' chances)

* violence (where they are inflicting violence onto others)
* sentencing someone to a punishment of some kind or belittling them
* dreaming of being in a position of power; e.g., dreaming of being a king, queen, leader, or boss of some kind where they have dominance, status, and control over others in the dream.

Spirituality

By listening to our intuition and dreams, and trusting the signs we receive from the universe, we naturally open ourselves up to receiving ongoing guidance, support, and healing from our spirit guides in both the physical world and the dream realm. Dreams are a special way for our spirit guides to communicate with us. They will project thoughts, ideas, and knowledge into our subconscious mind and higher self, which will later appear through déjà vu, synchronicity, and intuitive thoughts. How we choose to react, listen, and follow through with the insight we have received is entirely up to us.

Those who practise regular meditation and mindfulness, are involved in positive spiritual practices, talk regularly with their spirit guides, and approach life with a sense of openness and respect for the universe, other people, Mother Nature, and the spirit world will often experience prophetic and phenomenal dreams. Those who walk the spiritual path in waking life may regularly encounter vivid dreams involving spiritual guardians, mystical realms, spirit animals, and glimpses of past lives and future events.

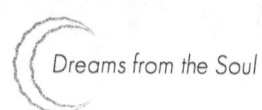

Dream symbols associated with our spiritual nature include:

- spirit animals and spirit guides
- spiritual realms and various universal planes
- deceased loved ones
- insight about the future (precognitive dreams are triggered by your higher self)
- memories of past lives
- receiving valuable advice or knowledge that you would not have otherwise known.

Physical body

When our body is lethargic, burnt-out, highly stressed, or riddled with illness, we enter a state of disharmony in our physical and metaphysical wellbeing. Our chakras become blocked, the ability to function at our highest potential diminishes, and our motivation and sense of patience is temporarily forgotten. Regardless of whether our physical ailments are considered small or large, the impact of bodily sickness, pain, and recovery naturally causes our dreams to take a peculiar and vivid turn.

It is incredibly common for people experiencing a high fever, passing flu, or suffering with a throat infection to dream of monsters, demons, flashing bright colours, and have chaotic, vivid, and intense dream themes appear.

Personal experience

When I had tonsillitis a few years ago, I repeatedly dreamt of demons and distorted figures who were suffocating and choking me. My dreaming experiences were heightened, and strong bold colours including red, black, and yellow kept appearing.

Dream symbols associated with the physical body include:

✶ When a person's health is in a positive and energised state, common dream symbols that will appear are: large, healthy green trees; the earth's floor (specifically bright-green grass, rich dirt, and vibrant landscapes); the sun; positive physical activity, including dancing, stretching, and sporting events; and having a lot of strength and vitality.

If someone has poor health, such as an autoimmune disease, the flu, or a bodily injury, their dreams may feature symbols such as an inability to move, bypass, or overcome objects, being drugged or sluggish, the presence of a doctor's office, hospital, or medical professional, and vivid, unusual, and intense dream themes.

✶ Animals (mammals in particular). Animals have a distinct metaphoric connection to our physical body and health status. E.g., if a dreamer is feeling physically rundown and sick in waking life, their body will symbolically project their tiredness and unwellness into the dream realm using an animal metaphor, such as seeing a wounded tiger or trying to care for an exhausted dog.

The relationship and bond that humans share with animals is a unique and powerful one. We consciously acknowledge and have witnessed firsthand that, like us, animals grieve over loss, they need love, care, and kindness to thrive, and when they are sick, they will come to us for help or retreat into themselves. The similarities between animals and

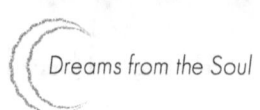

humans are undeniable, and that is why animals are often projected into the dream realm for matters of physical health and personality characteristics. Pay attention the next time you dream of an animal and try to recall how it was presenting itself because it may have insight to offer about your wellbeing.

Dream experience

Below is an 'animal' themed dream that was passed on to me from a lovely lady. During the time she experienced this dream, she was becoming increasingly overburdened and physically drained by the amount of work her new job role required her to complete.

I'm walking beside an elephant at a slow pace. We started off by walking down a path, but the elephant soon turned and changed directions and we walked to three grassy hills.

From this dream I immediately noticed three key symbols:

- Walking at a 'slow pace' beside the elephant:
  - Reflects the dreamer's need to physically slow down and take care of her body.
- Turning and 'changing directions':
  - Symbolic of making decisions, choices, and reprioritising life objectives and/or routines.
- Walking to 'three grassy hills':
  - Represents finding space, openness, and freedom.

- ☾ Grounding oneself and reconnecting with nature (element of earth).
- ☾ The number three symbolises collaboration, delegation, teamwork, and support.

Interpretation

When we intuitively interpret this dream, we can see the dreamer is physically pushing herself too far, with the high workload she needs to complete for her job. This is beginning to have a negative impact on her body, and she needs to 'slow her pace down'. This will require her to reconsider what 'choices or changes' she can implement to help lighten her workload. This may involve establishing a new routine/approach to her high workload, or reaching out to others (e.g., work colleagues or loved ones) for support and assistance, so she can more effectively manage her time and energy. She needs to reconnect and listen to her body by spending time in nature with the energy of spirit earth.

CHAPTER 5

Colours in Dreams

The colours that appear in someone's dreams will provide insight into their personality, how they relate to others, and how they see the world.

Many people attempt to interpret their dreams by relying solely on the major themes or symbols that took place in the dream vision. Although undoubtedly it is important to explore the main themes from your dreams, and often they are the 'key' to identifying the underlying context and meaning behind your dreams, the presence of dream colours can prove to be an asset in the interpretative process. Colours can reflect the state of a dreamer's wellbeing, stress levels, thought patterns, the relationships they share with others, the energy flowing through their chakras, and any life situations they are dealing with.

The next time you write down your dreams in your journal, ensure you take note of any repetitive colour themes that seem to surface. Learning to collectively combine all the elements and themes from your dreams, such as the colours, archetypes, symbols, and your emotional reaction upon awakening, will help provide greater depth and clarity regarding what your dream is trying to convey to you. Allow 'everything' from your dreaming experience to intuitively guide you with your interpretation.

Colour dream example

If an individual's dreams keep featuring shades of blue, we know this beautiful colour symbolises 'spirit of water, emotions, feelings, relaxation, spirituality, and fluidity'. The insight from this colour can automatically tell us that the dream is arising from an emotional and intuitive state rather than the ego, logical mind, or creative imagination.

Below you will find a general guide to dream colours and their meanings. If you feel that a certain colour has a different meaning for you compared to what has been written, then follow your instincts as there is never a right or wrong answer!

Dream colour meanings

- **Orange:** good health, energy levels, opportunities, excitement, surprise, gifts, and the Sacral Chakra.
- **Red:** passion, vitality, love, romance, ego, anger, confidence, sex, self-expression, and the Root Chakra.
- **Pink:** honesty, innocence, memories, self-love, childhood, and simplicity.
- **Purple:** imagination, spirituality, psychic gifts, creativity, deep thinking, philosophical thoughts, personal growth, and the Third Eye/Crown Chakra.
- **Yellow:** happiness, motivation, encouragement, uplifting thoughts, foundational security, abundance, spontaneity, and the Solar Plexus Chakra.
- **Green:** escape, adventure, clear thinking, nature, rebirth, new direction, freedom, opportunity, movement, and the Heart Chakra.
- **Blue:** possibilities, intuition, uncertainty, calmness, emotions, unconscious, spirituality, rest, relaxation, introspection, and the Throat/Third Eye Chakra.
- **Brown:** grounding energy, physical body, connectedness to nature, boredom, and reflection about life direction.

* **Black:** endings, new beginnings, death, liberation, shadow self, unconscious mind, and stressed/clouded/negative thoughts.
* **White and lilac:** harmony and balance in the mind, body and spirit, clear focus, spiritual protection, and following the right path.

CHAPTER 6

Precognitive Dreams

The future is forever evolving, shifting, and changing. The only thing we can control is how we react and respond to the experiences the universe lays before us.

Have you ever dreamt of something before it occurred? Perhaps you glimpsed into the future and saw a significant or mundane event that later unfolded, such as a natural disaster, death of a loved one, pregnancy, job opportunity, or the arrival of news.

The phenomenon of precognitive dreaming has been recorded since the beginning of humankind. Over the centuries and across all countries, prophets, fortune tellers, seers, psychics, shamans, spiritualists, and everyday people have dreamt of future events that later came true. With precognitive dreaming, the dreamer may experience the exact future event/outcome as what they saw in their dream. On other occasions, slight differences and variations from their precognitive dream will unfold, and other times the dreamer will physically change the outcome of what they saw in their dream vision (this is especially evident if the precognitive dream was a warning of some kind, and the outcome itself could be influenced and changed by the individual).

Why do we have precognitive dreams?

Precognitive dreams arise from a place of inner-awareness or, more specifically, from our higher self and spirit guides. I was recently asked by someone if there was a way they could train their mind to start having dreams about the future. In all honesty, I am not aware of any techniques that will help to invoke precognitive dreams, besides developing your psychic abilities. I believe that what you see in the dream realm depends on the relationship you share with your higher self, spirit guides, and the universe. Precognitive dreams seem to appear randomly and for varying reasons for every individual. One person may always dream of future pregnancies for those around them, someone else may dream of conversations that will soon take place, or another person will dream of a news story weeks before it occurs.

An interesting notion about precognitive dreaming is that the exact same or a slightly different dream scenario can be dreamt by two or more people. In the cases of unexpected natural disasters or significant events in history (such as the sinking of the *Titanic*), dozens of people reported having dreams with similar details to one another in the weeks and days leading up to the major event. In the case of terrorism attacks, or when an immense number of human lives are lost, the number of 'mutually shared' precognitive dreams, feelings of unsettledness, unexplained fear, overwhelming emotion, and the intuitive sense that 'something bad' is going to happen increases profoundly amongst society.

How and why does this occur?

Although no definite answer can be offered about precognitive dreaming, the reason in my mind is quite simple. We are all interconnected beings who can tap into the energy and knowledge that resides within our collective consciousness and universe. When major events occur throughout the world that result in chaos, loss of life, devastation, hardship, violence, and fear, our higher self 'instinctively senses and intuitively knows' that an impending detrimental event is going to occur.

Personal experience

I am going to share two examples where I experienced precognitive dreaming, which later proved to be accurate and true.

The first experience was a few months ago, when I had a precognitive dream about the train I regularly catch into the city to attend university. In the dream, *the train was running extremely late and caused me to miss out on an important lecture.*

I woke up in the middle of the night and automatically wrote the dream down in my journal. I also set my alarm so I could catch an earlier train, instead of the one I usually took. From the moment my alarm went off in the morning, I was extremely stressed and flustered because I knew I was going to be late to class. Shortly after I arrived at the train station, there was an announcement that the train was delayed due to technical issues. The train ended up being delayed for 45 minutes and then, halfway into the two-hour journey, the train had another malfunctioning issue. The entire train journey took close to three hours. When I arrived at campus, just as my dream predicted, I missed out on valuable lecture material.

We can see that in this instance I tried to change the outcome of what my precognitive dream showed me, by leaving earlier to catch another train. I instantly assumed upon awakening from the dream that *I* would be the reason for being late to class because I would miss my train. However, running late to class that day proved to be completely out of my control, and there was nothing I could have done to change the prediction from my dream.

 *Dreams from the Soul*

My second experience of precognitive dreaming involved several instances where I dreamt that someone I loved and cared for was going to die. Precognitive dreams about death are extremely upsetting because I know they will come true within two to three weeks. I experienced my first precognitive dream of death back in 2018, and I have since experienced these another three times. All these deaths were not expected and occurred suddenly, without warning. Each dream differed regarding what was shown to me, and I did not see what the cause of death would be. Instead, I experienced on average three to four precognitive dreams leading up to the death of a loved one, and I felt an immense amount of emotion and noticed signs from spirit around me.

I do not fear death, neither do I believe that it symbolises the eternal 'end' for the person or animal who passes away. In fact, I believe death is beautiful and simply signifies a transition from our world to the spirit world. In saying this, however, when I have precognitive dreams that someone I love is going to die, it is extremely upsetting and difficult for me. Although I believe it is a gift to have this precognitive ability, and I feel it is my spirit guides' way of helping me, it is still an enormous shock when they occur. When I dream of death, I experience what I can only describe as a 'heaviness' that weighs down my heart, mind, and energy until the physical death of my loved one occurs.

CHAPTER 7

Recurring Dreams

*Until we hear what needs to be heard,
we will be asked to listen.*

Visualise the image of a maze…

The maze will never end until you find the right direction, and this may take a long time.

There are many possible paths you can take, and you may become discouraged at times and feel there is no way out.

You will eventually find the right path and realise you knew the way out all along.

Recurring dreams follow the same principle as running around a maze and looking for clues to the way out. However, instead of a physical maze, the maze is located within your collective consciousness.

Recurring dreams transpire when your higher self and spirit guides are trying to gain your undivided attention.

Whether repetitive dreams occur in a short timeframe or sporadically throughout your lifetime, it is an evidently clear sign that something is failing to be acknowledged. This may be a beneficial change that needs to be implemented regarding career, finances, personal habits, and relationships. It could be a warning or serious wake-up call for your actions, morals, life choices, or the need to let go of karmic, emotional, and mental burdens. Other times, it can be a message to pursue new pathways, destinations, and creative interests.

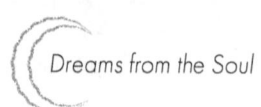

If you are someone who experiences recurring dreams, it is a good idea to reflect on what is happening in your life when the repetitive dream surfaces. You may establish a link between a certain person, environment, obstacle, or occasion that triggers your repetitive dream to arise. If you do not immediately recognise a link between your dreams and life situations, then consider the state of your mind and thought patterns in the days leading up to your recurring dream. For example:

* Were you feeling anxious, lonely, worried, or uncertain about the future?
* Have you been unhappy with yourself, or reflecting on how much you despise your job and wish you could do something different?

Rest assured, regardless of whether you can pinpoint the trigger for your recurring dreams, you can still discover the meaning behind them.

How to decipher your recurring dreams

First and foremost, ensure you journal absolutely everything that you can recall from your recurring dream, every time you dream it. You may notice the dream is identical every time, discover slight variations in the themes or archetypes, or notice varying emotional responses and thoughts that are triggered in you each time the dream unfolds. The ability to decipher a recurring dream lies in the repetitive details you come to recognise and the impact it has on your mindset and heart.

When you experience a recurring dream, ask yourself the following questions:

✳ Who are the people in your dreams?

☪ Consider the attitude, persona, and physical appearance of the people in your recurring dream.

✳ Can you identify who they are based on the people you know, or perhaps they remind you of someone from your past?

☪ Do you like the people in your dream? How do they treat you? What type of response do they trigger in you?

☪ Are they trying to teach you something? Does their behaviour mirror your own? Or, are there certain traits from the dream archetypes that you would like to develop in yourself?

✳ Is the scenery familiar?

☪ Pay attention to where your recurring dream is taking place and whether the scenery or location changes each time you experience the dream.

☪ Do you recognise the location? Is it your old childhood home, school, a place in nature, somewhere you have travelled to, or a destination you have never physically been before; e.g., another country or era of time? (Note: having recurring dreams of a place you have never been before, such as a different country or era of time, can often be a memory from a past life.)

☪ How does the scenery in your recurring dream make you feel? Are you scared, nervous, blissful, excited, want to leave, feel trapped or have a sense of freedom?

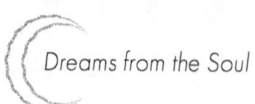
Dreams from the Soul

- ✳ What energy does the recurring dream carry?
  - ☾ Are there a lot of things happening in your dream, such as loud noises, chaos, messiness, lots of people, work to complete, deadlines, obstacles? Are you tripping over things, or running from something?
  - ☾ When you are experiencing stress and overthinking in waking life, this disorganised and restless energy will be projected into the dream realm. If you notice your recurring dream seems to occur around the time of a deadline or challenging life event, or when your anxiety, sense of worth, and self-confidence are suffering, then you can pinpoint that the recurring dream is being triggered by your mindset and stress levels.

- ✳ What are you striving for in your recurring dream (what is important to you)?
  - ☾ When recurring dreams feature the themes of performances, positive public recognition, having a special talent, climbing, or studying for an exam, these can be symbolic indicators relating to personal/ambitious/creative/business aspirations in waking life.
  - ☾ Pay attention to recurring dreams that feature themes involving the concept of 'striving towards something, achieving successful results, or discovering something new' because it can be your intuition guiding you to recognise new paths, skills, and opportunities around you.

✷ What is bothering you?
- ☾ Is there a specific trigger in your recurring dream that causes you anguish, frustration, sadness, or excitement?
- ☾ If you experience dissatisfaction in life, struggle to find happiness, or have never followed through with making positive changes and decisions to improve the quality of your life, then your psyche may project the following metaphors in your recurring dreams: being locked up, abandoned, restrained, not reaching your destination, missing public transport, mindlessly wandering in a deserted location, and being lost with no sense of direction. Recurring dreams such as these mirror the mental blocks that hold you back in life and the challenges or situations you want to leave behind.

Recurring dreams can arise for numerous reasons, including spiritual growth, past life energy, karmic debts, bad life choices, significant change that needs to occur, crisis of faith, unfinished business, lack of guidance, discovery of new beginnings, inability to find the right path, and not recognising (or following) the signs and synchronicity that is being left by the universe for you. It is only when you truly grasp a recurring dream's message, and integrate the guidance that is being passed on to you, that the dream itself will change immensely or cease completely from recurring.

Below, I have included recurring dreams that were passed on to me from two individuals, who granted me permission to include them in my book.

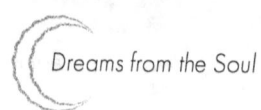
Dreams from the Soul

Recurring dream experiences

Dreamer one

A lovely tarot client of mine contacted me regarding a recurring dream she had been experiencing for the past three years, at least once a month. My client revealed she had tried to interpret the dream a few times, using dream websites and books, but could never find anything that resonated or made sense to her. She was initially hesitant to share the dream with me because she felt it was peculiar, but I assured her that all dreams are usually quite odd in context.

> *I'm sitting on the toilet in public, usually in view of others who ignore me, and there is no toilet paper to use. I don't know what to do and have no help.*

When analysing a dream, I begin by breaking down the key symbols:

* Toilet:
  * Privacy, solitude, and releasing what is no longer needed from the body.

* Being in view of the public (others):
  * Lack of privacy, exposure, openness, self-expression, vulnerability, judgement, and attention.

* Lack of toilet paper:
  * Uncertainty, vulnerability (notice this word has appeared twice in two symbols), hesitation, embarrassment, and a need to ask someone for help.

Using the breakdown of symbols and allowing my intuition to guide me with the interpretation process, I concluded my client's recurring dream was stemming from an emotional and/or mental source, rather than an external situation. The overlap of 'vulnerability' and holding back from asking someone for toilet paper (help) symbolises hesitation to vocalise what needs to be said aloud to someone/others. The recurring symbol of the 'toilet' signifies the importance of expelling and letting things go. Intuitively, I kept feeling that my tarot client had an emotional matter (matter of the heart) that needed to be dealt with and moved on from, once and for all.

After passing on the interpretation to my client, she responded with immense gratitude! She explained that everything made sense and aligned closely with an unfinished emotional situation between her and another individual.

Dreamer two

I was having a conversation with a work colleague one day and the topic of dreams came up. She went on to explain that she had been frequently experiencing a recurring dream for the past six months and could not figure out why it was happening. I was not close with this work colleague at the time and knew nothing of her personal life, but I asked her if she would like me to interpret her recurring dream for her, and she said yes.

I'm standing alone on the shore where the sand meets the water and I'm looking at a large ocean. I begin to feel extremely anxious and know that something bad is about to happen when I see the waves rising. All I can do is stand there and wait for the inevitable. The ocean soon

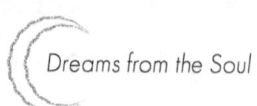

takes the form of a large tsunami, and it drags me under the water where I struggle not to drown.

I begin by breaking down the key symbols:

- Ocean:
  - Emotions, intuition, spiritual cleansing, purification, unconscious, freedom, and the element of water.
- Tsunami:
  - Disaster, emotional/mental/spiritual/physical breakdown, impending change, instincts, restlessness, movement, and the element of water.
- Extreme anxiousness:
  - Reflection of anxiety being experienced in real life, trepidation, disharmony in chakras and mindset, and fear of the future (unknown).
- Being dragged under water and struggling not to drown:
  - Feelings of helplessness, overpowering/overwhelming thoughts or life situation, and lack of support.
- Waiting for the inevitable:
  - Intuition, acceptance, change, and realisation of what is going to occur.
- Standing on the beach/shore where the water meets the sand:
  - Earth and water elements.
  - This detail from the dream is crucial! The connection between the two elements (dreamer is standing in both water and sand) highlights that the dreamer is 'currently' dealing with a situation in her life.

If she was to dream that she was standing far away from the water's edge, then this would change the context of the dream and could potentially mean that the situation has not yet come to light in the dreamer's life, or she is not yet ready to deal with the situation. Likewise, if she was to dream that she was swimming calmly in the water before being struck by the tsunami, this could indicate her unconscious awareness of the 'freedom and emotional healing' that will occur once her situation has been dealt with. If there was a symbol of a boat, life vest, or object that she could hold on to in the water, this would reflect the supportive role of other people in her life.

Once again, I allowed my intuition and the dream symbols to guide me with the interpretation process. I felt the recurring dream was related to a significant impending life change (tsunami), which would momentarily cause disruption and invoke a powerful emotional response in my work colleague (struggling not to drown). Deep down she already knows this change is inevitable (standing where the water meets the sand) and it causes her great anxiety as she cannot prevent it from occurring because it has been approaching for the past few months when the dream first started occurring.

I shared my interpretation with my work colleague, and she could not believe how accurate the interpretation was. She immediately related the interpretation to the difficulty she was experiencing in her relationship with her partner. She knew the relationship was coming to an end and she had to walk away from her marriage because her happiness and mental health depended on it. Fast-forward a couple of months and she found the inner strength to file for a divorce. The recurring dream has never appeared since.

CHAPTER 8

Awakening Dreams

I can never decide whether my dreams are the result of my thoughts or my thoughts the result of my dreams.
~ DH Lawrence

Have you ever had a dream that suddenly opened your eyes about something? Perhaps a dream that prompted newfound revelations, sparked sudden interest in following a new path, or provoked you to start thinking more deeply and philosophically about the world and your purpose in it?

Awakening dreams are experiences that subconsciously guide us to shift our behaviour, beliefs, priorities, decisions, and life perspectives. They affect us on a psychological and spiritual level and carry a powerful intention to help invoke personal and life revelations. Awakening dreams help us gain a clearer perspective on what is blocking us from our destiny and what we aspire to do in our life. Psychologically, awakening dreams can trigger us to recognise our character faults, fears, anxieties, strengths, inner resources, and skills. Spiritually, they will reveal elements from within our collective consciousness and higher self.

Awakening dreams are the 'link' between manifestation and reality and denote the beginning of a new chapter unfolding within our lives. This symbolic chapter may be undesired or welcomed with open arms, but despite our feelings towards the impending change, we need to accept that what happens next is part of our destiny. We experience many chapters throughout our life journey with different purposes, experiences, and lessons to learn. Awakening dreams will occur when your

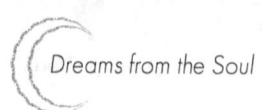

higher self and spirit guides want you to recognise that such universal shifts will soon take place in your future.

Despite the powerful impact awakening dreams can have, there are countless people who will disregard, underestimate, or second-guess what their dream shows them. For example, an individual may have an awakening dream that highlights the vital importance of ending a toxic friendship, so a deeper relationship with their partner can occur without being interfered with. However, the individual chooses to ignore the warning from the dream, and soon the friend causes their relationship to break down and end.

> *Awakening dreams can be the universe's way of steering us in the right direction to avoid unnecessary challenges.*

The difference between awakening dreams and regular dreams is that awakening dreams will have a lasting impact in your memory, not only upon awakening but for the days, months, and possibly years to follow. When you experience an awakening dream, you will never have to try to interpret what message is being conveyed to you. You will immediately understand its meaning and what aspect of your life or self it relates to. Awakening dreams can be described using the words 'concise, clear, loud, blunt, powerful, transformative, and revolutionary'.

At the end of the day, we all have freewill and the power to make our own decisions. But when awakening dreams occur, it can be the universe's way of trying to steer us in the right direction and avoid unnecessary challenges that we do not need to experience.

Awakening dreams may invoke the following:

* A sudden and strong urge to focus closely on a specific area of your life; e.g., spiritual development, business, artistry, or health, despite having no prior interest in doing so before the awakening dream occurred.
* A shift in your mentality that results in reassessing who you are, whether you are honouring your beliefs and morals, and questioning your place in the world and why you are here.
* A warning of impending misfortune, challenges, or illness from a spirit guide or dream archetype. (Precognitive dreams often coincide with awakening dreams.)
* An unexpected, strong urge to change self-destructive behaviours, move on from abusive relationships and toxic environments, etc. (Awakening dreams can serve as powerful wake-up calls for troubling life situations.)
* An opportunity to open your eyes to something you have been neglecting and developing the inner strength to suddenly confront it.
* A major life change; e.g., pursuing an entirely different career path or moving overseas.

Universal dream symbols

Like with all dreaming experiences, there is no 'one meaning' for a dream symbol or metaphor that will resonate with all of us. We all have different experiences, feelings, and connections to certain attributes, colours, archetypes, themes, etc. Awakening dreams are no different when it comes to this concept; however, there are four universal symbols that often

occur for 'similar' reasons for many people and will frequently appear in awakening dreams.

The four universal symbols are:
1) The world
2) Justice scales and judge's gavel
3) Crossroads
4) Human skull

Let us examine what these powerful symbols represent in the dream realm.

The world

Wherever you go in the world, carry kindness and gratitude in your heart.

Various metaphors may be used to represent the world in our dreams, but the three most recognisable symbols are: The World tarot card, a world globe, and seeing the world from an out-of-space perspective. To see the symbol of the world in your dreams is one of the most encouraging and uplifting signs the universe can send you!

Dreams featuring The World tarot card can signify physical and spiritual growth, entering a new stage in your life journey, emerging changes, and following your passions. If you dream of floating through space peacefully and seeing the world below you, it denotes open-mindedness, that future planning is essential, and positive opportunities will soon become available to you. Dreaming of a world globe symbolises having faith in the unknown, taking calculated risks to pursue dreams, developing new relationships, overseas travel or work is favoured, and new ventures are ready to be pursued.

World dream meanings:

* Needing to make long-term decisions, which will ultimately change the course of the dreamer's future.
* Contemplating life direction and soul purpose.
* Travel is beckoning.
* Aspirations and goals are achievable so continue investing your energy, time, effort, and hard work.
* Looking for opportunities or ways to change your current life situation.
* Needing to see things from a higher perspective.
* Certain aspects within the dreamer's waking life are coming to an end and they do not know what to do next; e.g., existential crisis, approaching retirement, divorce, relationship problems, being fired from a job, starting a new career path, graduating from school or university.
* Seeking or being ready for ambitious ventures and pursuing new paths.
* Birth (in the context of physical, spiritual, creative, material, etc.).

Justice scales and judge's gavel

To encounter either one or both symbols in the dream realm signifies logic, planning, and that a forward-thinking approach needs to be integrated into waking life.

From a spiritual and literal perspective, the judge's gavel and justice scales serve as the ultimate karmic reminder that what goes around will always come around, tenfold. To foresee

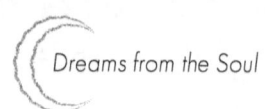

such an imperative symbol in the dream realm will require you to honestly reflect on everything that has recently happened in your life. Specifically, you should focus on any issues that involve the concept of loss, failure, deception, unjust situations, trickery, fraud, or any scenarios in which harsh words and regrettable actions took place and were not rectified.

The presence of the judge's gavel or justice scales in your dream can symbolise both a blessing and a warning depending on how you treat others and the world. Just as karma can provide a profound sense of relief and liberation to some, it can also be an unwelcome and heavy burden to those who have done wrong and need to learn the hard way that all actions have consequences.

For example, if you were to experience unjust business hardship, due to your work colleague being involved in fraudulent dealings and financial theft, then seeing the authoritative symbol of a judge's gavel or justice scales in your dream would invoke a positive sense of relief and confidence knowing that karma will soon prevail in your favour. However, it is a completely different interpretation if you are the one who chose to act unethically and created misery for those around you. In such a case, if a judge's gavel or justice scales appeared before you in a dream, it would serve as a powerful reminder that you could soon face the universal repercussions that are headed for you.

Justice scales and judge's gavel dream meanings:

* Receiving karmic intervention.
* Realising your negative traits; e.g., unhealthy habits, discriminatory views, manipulative behaviour, treating others with a lack of respect.

* Making smart decisions that will positively influence your long-term future.
* Believing in yourself and your ability to accomplish the goals and aspirations you have set for yourself.
* Receiving welcome and/or overdue news that brings reassurance and relief.

Crossroads

When you find yourself at a crossroads, look down at your feet and see what direction you are unconsciously stepping towards.

There is a vast number of legends and spiritual rituals that refer to the profound power and magical ability that a crossroads possesses. It is believed the 'crossroads' is where someone can go to change the fate of current and future life situations, release emotional baggage from the past, contemplate impending life decisions, dispel bad luck, call upon the spirits who inhabit the crossroads for assistance in spell work, and alter the direction your life is travelling in.

Traditionally, before you can work with the potent energy of the crossroads, you must make an offer to appease the spiritual beings who inhabit the crossroads (the four directions). This may be an offering of flowers, fruit, alcohol, cigars, or a personal item that you are willing to trade for the guidance and life opportunities you are seeking. In the case of the crossroads appearing as a dream symbol, the underlying power and ability to transform your life is no less significant.

Please ensure you pay your respects to the spirit world upon awakening from a crossroads dreaming experience. To express your gratitude, simply call upon your spirit guides and

Dreams from the Soul

thank them for their blessing and the opportunity to work with the energy of the crossroads.

Encountering the crossroads in the dream realm serves as a clear message from the universe that change is imminent, waiting to be discovered, or needs to be implemented into your life. Depending on the individual, the crossroads can represent a warning or insightful guidance regarding the dreamer's destined path and the choices they need to make.

Crossroads dream meanings:

* Support from the universe and spirit world.
* New cycles of energy, relationships, and career opportunities will soon arrive.
* Warnings and insight about impending decisions that need to be made.
* Transformation and discovery of personal potential.
* Releasing what holds you back.
* Stepping out of your comfort zone and considering all the options available to you.
* Unfolding destiny and fate.

Human skull

Contrary to popular belief, dreaming of a human skull neither foretells the looming death of yourself or loved ones, nor signifies bad luck, misfortune, and illness. When a human skull appears in the dream realm or during a meditative state, it is considered a spiritually symbolic experience, especially if the skull communicates with you!

Throughout history, human skulls have been perceived as the ultimate vessels of ancient wisdom, knowledge, and supernatural powers. Dating back to ancient civilisations, human skulls have been used in various spiritual rituals and ceremonies for numerous reasons, including spiritual enlightenment, protection, divination, conjure work, and contacting the deceased and spiritual deities.

The capacity for directed thinking I call intellect; the capacity for passive or undirected thinking, I call intellectual thinking. ~ CARL JUNG

When a human skull is encountered on a vision quest, astral journey, or in the dream realm, it can be a vessel for either a malevolent or benevolent spiritual being. Therefore, it is important to trust your intuition regarding how the human skull's presence makes you feel, the energy surrounding your vision, and what insight is being passed on to you. The projection of a human skull can also reflect your higher self (unconscious mind/psyche).

Human skull dream meanings:

* A certain cycle in your life is coming to an end. The end is inevitable (and may be abrupt or unexpected) but it is beneficial and necessary for you to move on from this chapter in your life.
* A powerful time for invoking deeper meditation experiences, past-life recall and spiritual development.
* Any difficulties and uncertainties you have been experiencing will soon pass; however, you must call upon

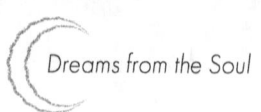

your inner strength, resilience, and motivation to help you overcome the last of your challenges.
- ✹ A time of healing ancestral, generational, and soul trauma.
- ✹ Connecting with spiritual beings.

Personal experience

I experienced a 'recurring awakening dream' that took place over the course of three weeks, which led me to discover my spirit power animal, develop a deep fascination of dreams, and guided me to embark on my tarot reading journey. It is important to note that I had no interest and little understanding of tarot divination, had never tried to connect with my spirit power animal prior to this event, and had never written down a dream before in my life! I undoubtedly owe this book and my tarot reading business to my spirit guides and power animal, for gifting me with such an incredible recurring and awakening dream experience.

If you have an open heart to the universe, you will awaken.

CHAPTER 9

Dreams of the Deceased

Death is not the end; it is simply a change of worlds.
A transition between the physical and spiritual.
Love always remains.

Have you ever dreamt of a deceased loved one? During our life, we form remarkable soul connections with various people. These special bonds and relationships do not cease to exist when they pass away. When someone we love and care for dies, although physically we can no longer hold their hand or have a conversation with them, the soulful bond and connection we share with them is still strongly present.

The grieving process that follows the death of a loved one is a powerful experience that impacts us in every way imaginable. For some, the experience of losing a loved one has the potential to trigger an existential crisis (loss of meaning or breakdown of faith), developing a sudden dependency on unhealthy coping mechanisms, loss of identity, inability to perform daily tasks and function healthily, and sadly there are those who never truly recover from the heartbreak and absence from losing their loved one.

I believe the concept of death, dying, and learning how to move forward in life without your loved one is unquestionably one of the most difficult experiences we as humans can go through. When pain, sadness, longing, denial, grief, and confusion surfaces when we are dealing with loss, our soul and broken heart need to feel and receive universal love. This is where dreams and the spirit world intertwine with each other and create the opportunity for passed loved ones to reconnect with us in the dream realm.

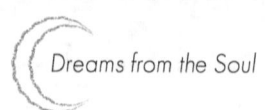

When grieving, many people will disconnect and isolate themselves from others because they feel they cannot (or do not want to) express how much pain they are truly feeling. This is when our dreams are incredibly helpful and healing as they allow the griever to connect with their spirit guides and passed loved one in an altered state of consciousness. This dreaming experience helps provide closure, healing, love, and comfort to the person in need.

There is a staggering number of people who report dreaming of their deceased loved one shortly before their actual time of death occurred and soon after they died. Some people are given a message from their deceased loved one in a dream, and others will see the spirit of their loved one looking healthy, at peace, and smiling once again, or wearing their favourite clothing. Others report being visited by their deceased loved one when they are struggling with hardships and life challenges, dealing with illness, or struggling to find a way forward.

The soulful bond we share with those we love is carried over into the spirit world when someone passes away. It is the profound love and connection that exists between people that ensures our deceased loved ones will always be a part of our life journey and will help guide us from a higher spiritual plane. When we encounter obstacles throughout our life, struggle to pick ourselves up to keep going, unconsciously seek answers, support, and guidance, and try to find reassurance that everything will be okay, sometimes we will not find or receive these things from other people. This may be due to a broken or non-existent support system, lack of community support, or perhaps the person we used to turn to during troubling times is no longer physically with us.

Those who report dreaming of their deceased loved one during times of crisis and great difficulty, recall feeling more uplifted, lighter in their body and mind, and have a renewed sense of motivation to keep moving ahead. In other words, the love and support a passed loved one used to offer us when they were alive does not cease to occur when they cross over into their spiritual form.

Did you know...

If there is a special life occasion such as a wedding, an announcement of pregnancy, the birth of a new baby in the family, or significant career or personal achievement, it is normal to experience increased signs of spiritual activity around your home and dreams involving passed loved ones.

CHAPTER 10

Dream Disorders

*I have had dreams and I have had nightmares,
but I have conquered my nightmares because
of my dreams.* ~ Jonas Salk

Parasomnia

The term 'parasomnia' is not one most people are familiar with. It categorises sleep disorders that fall into the classification of 'unbalanced and unusual reactions' that people can experience while sleeping. These reactions may include thrashing and jostling body movements, hallucinations, clutching the body as though in pain, talking aloud with jumbled speech or swearing, bouts of laughter, emotional reactions such as crying, fear, or anger, and having one-sided conversations.

If you are curious about what you do while you are asleep and dreaming, ask those you live with to write down or record anything they observe you doing during the night, or set up a voice recording dream app on your phone. I have recorded myself several times and it is quite fascinating to hear yourself say random words or laugh unexpectedly when you are asleep! Also, do not be alarmed if your voice sounds disorientated when you play back the recording, as your ability to coherently articulate words becomes more difficult in an altered state of consciousness.

Sleepwalking

Sleepwalking is a unique and peculiar disorder where a person who is sleeping can rise from their bed, walk around the house,

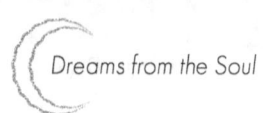

effectively navigate around furniture, and perform tasks such as cooking, cleaning, and changing their clothes. In their altered state of consciousness, sleepwalkers will not always register who is talking to them (such as a parent or spouse) and will have little to no recollection of their sleepwalking experience, upon awakening in the morning.

There is an old wives' tale that says you should not wake up a sleepwalker because they can become violent. However, if you approach a sleepwalker in a calm, controlled, and gentle manner, then generally you will not have a problem in guiding them back to bed while they remain in their altered state. The only time a sleepwalker may become violent or defensive with their words and bodily response is if they are experiencing a negative or frightening dream at the same time you are trying to awaken them (sleepwalkers reacting violently is not a common occurrence). So, whether you choose to completely wake up a sleepwalker or lead them back to the safety of their bed while they remain asleep, the decision is ultimately up to you.

Night terrors

Night terrors have a psychologically disturbing impact on a person's psyche, emotions, and mindset. The dreamer will experience terrifying dream scenarios, which cause them to verbally call out in distress, violently thrash and roll around in bed, activate the flight or fight bodily response, or awaken with strong emotional reactions such as fear, dread, terror, shock, and crying.

Many people confuse nightmares and night terrors because they are both frightening dream experiences. Although they both involve negative dream themes, night terrors have a substantial impact on the dreamer's mental health and can trigger a deep-rooted fear that stops them from wanting to fall asleep altogether because of what they may dream of. Night terrors feel incredibly real to the dreamer, and there are those who report feeling lifelike pain, suffering, and horror during their night terror episode.

Nightmares

Nightmares are a dreaming phenomenon that most people will experience at least once during their lifetime. Nightmares should not be confused with bad dreams as they are based upon the principles of violence, death, monsters, fear, danger, and themes that the dreamer finds frightening. Bad dreams, on the other hand, are more light-hearted in context and often involve scenarios such as walking around naked in front of people, failing an upcoming exam, doing something embarrassing, losing your favourite necklace, etc.

The theory behind nightmares is that they are triggered when an individual is intoxicated due to substance abuse, have consumed too much caffeine, are stressed out, overworked, suffering with poor mental health, or when a troubling life event is occurring; for example, divorce of parents, marital issues, sudden loss of job, financial bankruptcy, or abuse. However, what I find most interesting about this theory is that the majority of nightmares are experienced by young children. For argument's sake, if we consider young children as being the most sheltered from violence, war, terrorism, harm, and frightening situations, then why do they experience considerably more nightmares than adults, who are constantly bombarded with news stories of misfortune, sadness, violence, and terror?

My view (although I cannot validate it with proof) is that children are intuitively sensitive and soulfully aware of what is occurring in the environments and atmosphere around them. Children can instinctively recognise the energy of people and read body language cues, even if they do not understand the context of the interaction/conversation taking place. They can recall past-life memories in their dreams and are naturally more sensitive to spiritual activity and spiritual beings.

For those who have children, how many have experienced your child say, 'There's a monster in my room,' or, 'There's a monster in my dreams'? Now, how many of you can recall witnessing paranormal/spiritual activity when you were a child, or perhaps you had an imaginary friend? Young children are more receptive to vivid dreams, nightmares, past-life memories, and spiritual activity because there is nothing holding the young child's mind back from experiencing them. Unlike adults, who unintentionally block their clair-senses due to their mind being filled with numerous responsibilities, commitments, and stress.

Violent and frightening dreams

Ninety-nine percent of people at some stage in their life journey will experience a dream where violent tendencies, underlying threats, frightening themes, and aggressive qualities are present. In certain cases, these dream experiences may be categorised as night terrors or nightmares, as discussed earlier.

Certain people may dream of violence on a regular basis but have no violent inclinations in waking life, nor are they surrounded by violent situations. Whereas others may only dream of violent or frightening dream episodes when they are experiencing financial hardship, career problems, stress, mental and physical burnout, or relationship burdens. I want to make it clear to anyone who dreams regularly of violence, war, or fearful situations, to not feel like there is something wrong with you because you are not dreaming of sunshine, daisies, and rainbows.

Those who are naturally empathic, abuse survivors, living in dangerous environments, war veterans, police officers, counsellors who regularly listen to traumatic life stories, deep thinkers who question why bad things happen and try to find a reason behind it, and those who view the world with a glass half-empty attitude, have a higher chance of experiencing frightening, upsetting, and violent dreams.

As we mentioned earlier, children have a stronger recollection of past-life memories when they dream, without needing to be clinically regressed as most adults do. However, this is not to say that adults cannot experience unconscious memories of their past lives in the dream realm. In fact, if you find yourself always dreaming of a particular era in time, such as the 17th century, or a frightening event (e.g., running from warriors wielding swords, being under attack in a war, burning in fire), a specific country (you may dream vividly about a country despite never having travelled there), or continually see yourself as a different 'person' in the dream realm (different physical appearance, nationality, gender, or age, etc.), then you may well be tapping into past-life memories where you

experienced violence, trauma, or fear, and the memory has remained in your psyche.

How do you react to violence and fear in the dream realm?:

* Were you frozen in place and unable to move?
* Did you run faster to escape the impending doom that was getting closer?
* Did you break free from the cage or restraints you were being held in?
* Did you feel the pain that was being inflicted upon you?
* Did you fight back, get angry, or have superpowers to defend yourself?
* Did you cower, cry, or beg?
* Did you recognise the scary or violent dream character? Do they have similar characteristics or traits to anyone you know in waking life?
* Have you had this frightening dream before, is it recurring? And, if so, does it always remain the same or change slightly?
* Does the fear or violent themes in the dream seem familiar somehow? Is it triggering a sense of déjà vu in you?

We all react differently to violent and fearsome situations, whether this is in the dream realm world or physical world. In most individuals, the 'flight' instinct is triggered when the possibility or impending likelihood of danger, attack, threat, or violence is nearby. The flight instinct is often subconsciously triggered in the dream realm when we are experiencing a nightmare or night terror. Our automatic reaction is to awaken ourselves quickly and flee (flight instinct) from the terrifying dream scenario. Many individuals report jolting awake just before a violent act is inflicted upon them in the dream realm; for example, awakening just before being killed, drowned, stabbed, or tortured.

> *We cannot shield ourselves from everything negative and unsettling.*

Although the majority of us are naturally attuned with the instinct of 'flight' when threatening situations arise, there are those who are trained to 'fight' and eliminate the impending threat of danger (e.g., soldiers in war and law enforcement officers). These individuals are trained to approach danger head on and engage in battle, without experiencing the instinct to flee or freeze. Because they have been psychologically reprogrammed to react defensively and protectively of others, this will impact how they respond to violent and triggering dreams. Instead of trying to automatically wake themselves up or run away from the frightening dream situation, they will often try to fight back and defend the other dream characters that are present in their dream vision.

Triggers that can cause violent and frightening dreams:

* PTSD and painful memories of abuse, violence, and psychological trauma that was either witnessed or personally experienced.
* Visual or auditory sources (e.g., violence that is described or shown in movies, books, documentaries, song lyrics, podcasts, the news, and social media platforms that spread hate, racism, sexism, violence).
* Being in a domestic abuse household or toxic environment.

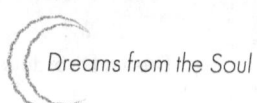

- ✳ Substance abuse/addiction.
- ✳ Physical burnout, bullying, psychological breakdown, and decline in mental health.
- ✳ Poor diet (e.g., consuming high amounts of sugars, saturated fat, and highly caffeinated beverages).
- ✳ Temper problems, impatience, narcissism, and feelings of extreme annoyance, rage, and resentment to either yourself or the world in general.

You could argue that violence is seemingly impossible to escape from in society. We cannot shield ourselves from everything negative and unsettling because once it has been seen, heard, discussed, or witnessed, it is imprinted within our subconscious mind, imagination, and memory and is later projected into the dream realm.

Violent dream example

Below is a hypothetical example of a violent dream that could be triggered by the subconscious mind recalling details of a violent news story.

> *An individual is watching the news, and the story of a violent war between two rival gangs is playing on the screen. The news presenter reveals that mutilation of the victims' bodies is a signature of the gangs, and while a shootout was occurring in the streets between the two gangs, a man and his young daughter were killed in the crossfire.*

Depending on a person's morals, personality type, and universal values, there are numerous ways their subconscious mind could project this story into the dream realm. I have written a potential dream scenario that could surface days, weeks, or months down the line for the individual.

Possible dream scenario

The dreamer is standing in the middle of a firing range, holding an injured and bloodied small deer. Suddenly, they become the target of several armed men who are dressed like hunters. Carrying the small deer, the individual tries to flee and jumps for cover into the surrounding shrubs, while the men shoot at them and wave their hunting knives in the air.

I have used various metaphors and themes in this hypothetical dream, just like our subconscious mind does with all our dreaming experiences. Now, let us break down the dream and see how it relates to the news story:

* The men dressed as 'hunters' represent the rival gang members.
* The environment of a 'firing range' symbolises a place where targets are hit.
* Holding a 'bloodied and injured small deer' showcases the dreamer's instinctive nature to protect those that are defenceless.
* The small deer is a symbolic metaphor of the 'young child' who was killed in the shootout.
* The 'guns' the dream characters are shooting with represent the ruthless and careless actions of the gang members that ended up causing the death of a father and his child.

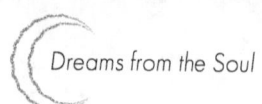

- The 'waving of the knives' is a detail the dreamer recalls from the news story when the reporter discussed how mutilation of the bodies was a signature of the gangs. The dreamer's subconscious mind has automatically linked knives as a tool used in mutilation.
- 'Diving into nearby shrubs for cover' highlights the dreamer's flight instinct was activated.

CHAPTER 11

Spiritual Dream Attacks

Close your eyes,
Look inside
Hear the answers from your ancestors.

Do you ever feel like something is watching you at night and causing you to feel unsettled? Have you felt threatened by an unseen force or spiritual being in the dream realm?

Spiritual attacks in the dream realm cannot be compared to any other dream disorder as the dreamer has little to no control over what they experience. Regular nightmares, night terrors, and flashbacks of past trauma are all, to a certain extent, triggered by subconscious recollection, imagination, and memories. However, spiritual dream attacks are caused by low-vibrating spiritual beings and entities who wish to inflict fear, suffering, and violence in the dream world. Like sleep paralysis, spiritual dream attacks often feature distorted and psychologically disturbing creatures (that cannot be defined as human or animal), violence that is directed towards the dreamer and/or is inflicted upon other dream characters, loud laughing or roaring, indecipherable language being spoken, and the intense feelings of danger and terror.

There is no second-guessing when a spiritual attack occurs in the dream realm! It is an incredibly frightening and memorable experience that is not in any way influenced by your imagination. Spiritual attacks come from a place of darkness, mischievousness, negativity, anger, and oppression from low-vibrating spiritual entities.

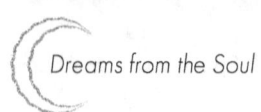

Dreams from the Soul

What are the triggers?

Although there are numerous reasons why we might experience a spiritual dream attack, I have identified two main triggers:

1) Spiritual curiosity
2) Mentality and behaviour

Spiritual curiosity

This relates to those who actively involve themselves in spiritual practices and rituals, including tarot cards, Ouija boards, astral journeying, hallucinogens, divination, spell work, conjure, seances, and automatic writing. By actively working with your psychic abilities and spiritual tools, you allow your connection and relationship to the spirit world to grow profoundly. Your clair-senses and intuition will begin to sharpen over time, and so does your ability to conduct accurate and insightful divination readings. Visions during meditation, astral journeying or scrying will become clearer and increasingly vivid as you ascend deeper into the spiritual realms. You may also notice increased spiritual activity and presences around you as you form a closer bond with your spirit guides and power animal.

The majority of people who become involved in spiritual work do so for positive reasons; for example, spiritual growth, seeking a deeper understanding of their life's purpose and the universe, personal development, to help guide or heal others, and because they have a genuine interest in learning about the paranormal. What some people do not initially realise, when it comes to working with the higher realms and using spiritual tools, is the acknowledgement that both 'good and bad' exists in the spirit world. Just as there are positive, loving, encouraging, and knowledgeable spirits that we can connect and work with, there are also malicious and negative spirits that we can potentially cross paths with during our spiritual journey. As our fascination and the desire to delve further into spiritual realms and divination practices grows, we make ourselves increasingly visible to the spirit world and the beings who reside within it. Ultimately, when we open our mind to the other side, we never know what type of spirit is looking back at us.

Mentality and behaviour

Our perspective towards life and how we behave and treat others, the environments we encounter, and the people we spend time with can significantly influence the universal and karmic energy that will surround us during our lifetime. What we project outwards into the world and internally to ourselves affects the relationship (sometimes non-existent relationship) we share with our spirit guides. When a lack of faith, gratitude, and respect is present in an individual's mind, it can have a detrimental impact if they were to encounter a malicious spiritual entity, in either the physical world or dream realm. They will not have the strength and power from their spirit guides to help them, and their own negative and cynical mentality will make it difficult to connect with white light positive energy.

The types of people who will unconsciously attract negative energy and spiritual entities towards them are:

- ✶ People who purposely inflict:
    - ☾ abuse and bullying

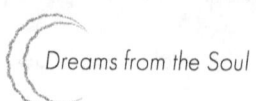

  - ☾ hardship and misfortune
  - ☾ pain.
- ✱ People who go through life with:
  - ☾ bitterness and hate
  - ☾ spitefulness
  - ☾ a strong judgement and discrimination towards others
  - ☾ jealousy and resentment
  - ☾ a lack of empathy for those suffering
  - ☾ a mocking attitude for all spiritual and religious beliefs
  - ☾ no remorse for their actions
  - ☾ blame towards everyone else for their own mistakes
  - ☾ a desire to manifest and project misfortune, illness, and evil energy onto others.

Have you ever noticed that bitter and hateful people seem to experience a lot of bad luck, opportunities do not work out for them, and they barely have anything good happen in their life? The negative energy a person sends out into the universe will always follow the law of attraction and be sent directly back to them. This will often be in the form of spiritual dream attacks, violent or mundane dreams, and bad luck that is influenced by low-vibrating spiritual entities.

If you create darkness in the lives of others and carry darkness within your mind and soul, then spiritual darkness will be drawn to you.

Prevention

There are a few precautionary steps you can take to help prevent spiritual dream attacks from occurring. You do not need to follow every step, just find what works for you!

- ✷ Chakra visualisation before drifting to sleep:
  - ☾ Imagine each of your seven chakras as colourful flowers or balls of light.
  - ☾ Starting from the Crown Chakra and working your way down to your Root Chakra, visualise that the petals of each chakra flower are curling inwards, or that the balls of light that represent each chakra are dimming down to a soft glow. Allow this exercise to take between 5 to 10 minutes to complete.

Note: if you struggle to remember the colours associated with each chakra, simply visualise a gold or white colour in your mind to represent them. The main objective of this exercise is to close down your chakras and ensure they are not open and receptive to unwanted spiritual energies. Closing down your chakras before you drift to sleep helps invoke spiritual protection for when you enter an altered state of consciousness and begin to dream. If you are interested in using the specific colours associated with each chakra, then see the following guide:

- ☾ Crown ~ violet
- ☾ Third Eye ~ indigo
- ☾ Throat ~ blue
- ☾ Heart ~ green
- ☾ Solar Plexus ~ yellow

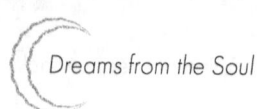

- ☾ Sacral ~ orange
- ☾ Root ~ red

* Spirit guides and universal white light energy:
  - ☾ Call upon your spirit guides (the spiritual deities or higher power you believe in) using prayer. Ask them to keep you safe and protected from negative energy in the dream realm by using their power, love, strength, and positive energy.
  - ☾ Visualise yourself as though you are cloaked in white light mist. Universal white light energy is the highest form of spiritual protection and can be called upon at any time to help cast out darkness, evil, and negative spiritual entities.

* Crystal energy:
  - ☾ Place protective crystals around your room, in your pillow, or wear them in the form of jewellery when you go to bed.
  - ☾ Ensure you program your crystals with the intent to deflect paranormal activity, spiritual dream attacks, and to promote peaceful sleep. (See Chapter 16 for a list of the most effective crystals for dreaming, spiritual protection, astral projection, and psychic development.)

* Mindset and body:
  - ☾ Release any anger, vengeful thoughts, jealousy, resentment, hate, and malice before you drift to sleep.
  - ☾ When you go to bed in an agitated mindset and carry tension in your body, your subconscious mind will naturally project this negative energy into your

dreams. If any low-vibrating spiritual entities are around, they will be drawn to your bitterness and unbalanced state.
- ☾ Try grounding yourself by standing outside under the cool night sky or do a guided meditation/deep-breathing practice for a few minutes before going to bed. These simple rituals will help to clear your mind, ground your spirit, and release any lingering stress and tension from your body.

* Psychic vampires:
  - ☾ Be mindful of the type of people you spend time with throughout your day.
  - ☾ Certain people will have incredibly intense, heavy, overly emotional, negative, unhappy, and burdened energy. We often refer to these people as 'psychic vampires' because they have the ability to unconsciously drain our energy and happy thoughts, trigger irritation, negativity and pettiness in us, and dysregulate our wellbeing.
  - ☾ Ensure you properly cleanse yourself after being in the company of such individuals, because other people's energy can remain attached to us. You may use the element of water (showering, bathing, swimming), smudging using white sage (see the tips for smudging below), grounding yourself outdoors in nature, aromatherapy, or crystals to clear the energy of psychic vampires.

* Spiritual burnout:
  - ☾ It is normal for people who provide spiritual services to others (e.g., a tarot reader, shaman, medium, reiki

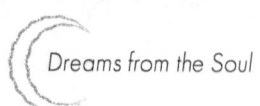

healer) to become physically drained or ill when they have pushed themselves too far with the amount of spiritual work they have been doing for others.

☾ Physical symptoms, such as dizziness, fatigue, and headaches, can be triggered when spiritual practitioners and healers overextend their spiritual energy to others. They become unbalanced in their metaphysical and physical body, and overly receptive to absorbing the energy of the clients they are working with.

Tips for smudging

White sage, also referred to as Grandfather Sage, is an ancient cleanser that can be used for ceremonies, cleansing sacred spaces (including your home, crystals, altar tables, divination tools), and for prayers. Native American cultures have used this natural method of cleansing and healing for thousands of years. White sage has a naturally calming effect for our senses, helps clear the air of bacteria, pollen and dust, promotes clearer mental focus and positive sleep, and offers spiritual protection from negative entities and ill-wishing from others. Here are some tips for smudging your home:

✳ Traditionally, a sage stick, natural feather, and abalone shell are used together. This combination helps to enhance the protection and powers of the white sage and your intentions. However, you can use the sage stick by itself. Ensure all your windows and doors are open before you sage your space as this allows the unwanted energies to leave your home.

✳ Light your smudge stick and gently blow to create the smoke.

- ✷ This will now be transferred to your surrounds to remove stagnant energy, evil, illness, and low vibrations.
- ✷ Walk to each room of your home to purify your surrounds with the smouldering sage.
- ✷ Speak your pure intent for cleansing your desired space such as, 'I clear this space of any spiritual presences,' 'I cleanse myself of anger and resentment,' 'I call upon the highest of healing and positive energy.'
- ✷ Use your feather (or breath) to disperse smoke to all corners of your home. If you wish to sage yourself or others to remove any stagnant, negative, or unbalanced energy, start from your head and work down to your toes, and use your feather (or breath) and allow the smoke to gently cleanse your spiritual and physical body.
- ✷ Always give thanks to Great Spirit and the universe for their presence, protection, and guidance.

Once cleansing has finished, extinguish your sage by putting it in sand or the earth. I usually leave mine to smoulder out naturally.

Personal experience

As a professional tarot reader, I offer my spiritual services to new and returning clients every week. On several occasions I have experienced 'overdoing' the amount of tarot readings I can comfortably and happily do, which has triggered my wellbeing to become unbalanced and unwell. When you provide spiritual services to others, you can easily push yourself too far because you naturally want to help as many people as possible when they reach out to you. Whenever you do spiritual work, not only are you using your own energy, but you are also connecting

and channelling the energy of your clients. Within my tarot reading career, I have encountered many psychic vampires and unhappy people who have caused me to feel physically ill during their reading, or for hours afterwards. It may be through no fault of their own that these individuals have such a low-vibrating energy and mentality, but simply that life has taken its toll on them, and they have given up.

I am going to share two different spiritual dream attacks; one several months ago and one a few years ago.

Spiritual dream attack one

The first spiritual dream attack occurred because I ignored my intuition when it told me I was doing too many tarot readings for clients. I had just started reading professionally, but I was overworked, in a state of disharmony, stressed out, suffering with a continual headache, and channelling the energies from my clients. I have since learned to recognise the signs my body is showing me, and no longer feel guilty about putting my wellbeing and mental health first.

The location in the dream was of a rural truck stop and petrol station, where I was wandering around lost. I instantly felt dark energy and danger surrounding me, and knew I had to find a way out of the place quickly. Suddenly, ghosts, dark shadows, and evil spiritual entities began surrounding me and started pulling at my arms, legs, and torso. No matter how hard I struggled, there were too many of them. The largest dark entity stepped forward and started laughing as it dragged me by my legs down through the concrete ground and kept dragging me deeper and deeper to the bottom of the world. I was terrified, and I instinctively knew, even in an altered state of consciousness, that this was not a normal dream, and if I ended up where this entity was taking me, it would truly hurt me.

I kept struggling and looking around for anything I could grab or hold onto, but all I could see was the soil, earth, and the emergence of fire when I looked down. I managed to yell out in the dream and wake myself up, but the moment I opened my eyes I was still being dragged and the entity was laughing at me. I had two more false awakenings until I was finally able to awaken properly. I did not go back to sleep that night because I knew the demonic entities were waiting for me. The entire time the spiritual dream attack was occurring, I knew I was being dragged to hell.

Spiritual dream attack two

The second spiritual dream attack was the result of dark magick (evil spirits) sent to me by a hateful and vengeful individual, who had no respect for her spirit guides and failed to believe in the power of karma. Without going into extensive detail, the woman was a spiritual fraud, alcoholic, and regularly noticed dark spiritual entities in her home. Having dark energy around you, being continually intoxicated, and providing spiritual divination and spell work for clients is not a joke and is incredibly dangerous for everyone involved. I informed her that what she was doing was blatantly wrong, and that lying to her clients about what she saw in their futures was a despicable and low thing to do. She did not take my words lightly and directed powerful dark magick to me in the dream realm, and it also affected my mother and father's dreams too.

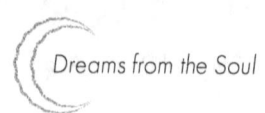
Dreams from the Soul

The details in my mind of this spiritual dream attack are not as clear as my other one, despite this experience only occurring recently. The reason being: I only wrote down a few sentences in my dream journal because I did not want to remember what I had seen during this dream. I also felt that if I wrote in extensive detail what had happened, it would be somehow holding on to the negative spiritual entities and energy that I encountered.

I dreamt of mutilation. Hundreds of bodies in front of me were being mutilated by dark spirits and men with deformed and twisted faces. I was trying to hide among the body parts, while willing myself to wake up from the dream, but it was not working. I cannot recall whether it was my arm or leg, but I vividly remember that a demonic man cut through one of my limbs with a machete and the pain was agonising. I was screaming in pain, while maggots and grubs were covering the floor, and I could only watch as the mutilation got worse and worse around me. I barely managed to wake myself up and, when I finally did, I was dripping in sweat despite it being winter. Every muscle in my body was tensed and cramped, and I was holding onto either the arm or leg that had been removed in the dream. I did not go back to sleep that night because what I saw in that spiritual dream attack was psychologically disturbing. For the next two days, I kept seeing a shadow silhouette in the corner of my eye throughout my house, and I knew something dark was around me.

Where it gets really interesting, however, is the fact that both my mum and dad had shocking dreams directly one day after me (I did not tell my family about my spiritual dream attack). My mother saw what she described as an 'evil black entity' who had a broom and long talon hands. The entity was sweeping away our family business and every possession in our home was missing. My mother believes the entity was pure and unmistakable evil, and she was terrified of the spiritual dream attack she experienced. My dad had a dream of a man who wanted to return an item he had purchased from our business and kept insisting he bring it to our house. When Dad saw the crystal the man wanted to return, he knew it was a bomb that was meant to kill us. He managed to throw the bomb just as it detonated. Now, my dad is someone who *never* remembers his dreams, so for him to recall the dream attack in such clarity was remarkable!

Mom and I both agreed that the spiritual dream attacks and the dark spiritual entity I kept seeing around the house had been manifested from the older woman and her hate towards me. We ended up smudging the house and called upon our spirit guides and the white light of protection to surround us all, and to deflect the evil energy that had been sent to us. Nothing else was experienced after the house was cleansed.

The most important advice I can pass on to anyone who is experiencing paranormal activity or spiritual dream attacks, is to not feed into the fear, panic, or anxiety as this will further increase the spiritual activity. Instead, focus your attention on smudging yourself and your home every day, call upon your spirit guides for help, close down your chakras before drifting to sleep, and raise your spiritual vibration.

Did you know...

The low-vibrating spiritual entities that appear in the dream realm do so with the intention of invoking fear, desperation,

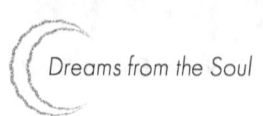

and inner turmoil within the dreamer. Every spiritual entity is unique and will be driven by their own motivation, desire, and intention. Sometimes, a spiritual entity may be drawn to a particular individual because they recognise a connection or similarity between themselves and the dreamer. For example, if a low-vibrating entity suffered with depression and suicidal ideation during their physical lifetime, and could not find peace when they passed away, there are instances when their emotional debris and unbalanced energy will follow them into the afterlife. These restless and negative entities are often drawn to individuals who are experiencing similar hardships and life troubles.

Spiritual dream attacks will leave you shaken and reiterate the deep and profound fact that we are never alone.

CHAPTER 12

Lucid Dreaming

To discover your authentic self is the most exhilarating and challenging journey you will experience in your lifetime.

Lucid dreaming is a fascinating experience! For most of us, when we dream it can feel as though we are watching a movie, but we cannot pause, rewind, or fast-forward because the dream itself is in control. For lucid dreamers, on the other hand, when they first enter the dream realm, or when they suddenly become aware that they are dreaming, they can begin influencing their dream self (the words they speak, how they interact with other dream archetypes, where they choose to explore, etc.) and in other cases can create a whole new dream scenario based on their imagination.

The practice of lucid dreaming provides us with the perfect opportunity to express ourselves freely and do things we normally could not do in the physical world; for example, being able to fly, having superpowers, changing the dream scenery to what you want it to be, breathing underwater, or walking without pain in our bodies. Those who are passionate and immerse themselves deeply in the practice of lucid dreaming, report noticing over time that their lucid dreaming abilities naturally develop and heighten to a significant degree.

Lucid dreaming is especially helpful and could almost be described as a 'breakthrough' for those who suffer with nightmares, violent dreams, and night terrors. Instead of allowing frightening and disturbing dreams to occur repetitively and hinder the dreamer's ability to sleep peacefully, if the individual can learn and master the art of lucid dreaming, they can begin taking back the control they were previously lacking

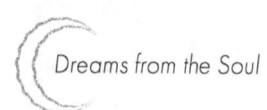
Dreams from the Soul

in the dream realm. Once realisation, power, and control can be gained in an altered state of consciousness, the individual can change their dreaming experiences into something more peaceful, positive, and beneficial to their mental and emotional state.

Have you experienced lucid dreaming?

There are several signs to indicate whether you have reached a lucid state in your dreams:

* Registering what your body looks like (acknowledging your limbs and physical appearance).

    In normal dreams, we rarely pay attention to what our body looks like. We do not look down to see our hands, tattoos, scars, piercings, body shape, hair colour, or any other physical attributes that define who we are and how we look. However, in lucid dreams the individual has more control over their body movements and can observe their dream form (body), if they so choose, although the details may be slightly blurred.

* Being able to influence and change dream factors, scenery, people, or situations.

    Rarely in regular dreams can we change the circumstances of what is occurring, and we do not realise or question the inconsistencies that are present. Lucid dreamers can recognise that what they are seeing is a dream and can begin changing the themes, scenery, and situations.

* Possessing extraordinary skills, such as having the ability to fly, levitate, or battle monsters with great strength and bravery.

With normal dreams we cannot run faster, despite trying our hardest to do so, and our ability to jump, hide, escape, fight, and yell is hindered dramatically. We are often left feeling 'stuck' and unable to influence our dreams how we want to.

* Entering the dream realm in a lucid state of mind, or unexpectedly realising that you are dreaming throughout the night.

   With regular dreams we do not consciously realise that we are dreaming, despite how far-fetched, vivid, and intense the dreaming experience may be.

Downfalls of lucid dreaming

I feel the need to address some common misconceptions about lucid dreaming. For some bizarre reason, there are quite a few negative opinions surrounding the idea that lucid dreaming is bad for our mental health, is dangerous, and has a paranormal component involved in it. Although I respect and appreciate everybody's varying ideas and opinions, I notice that many people base their negative lucid dreaming views on second-hand information shared from others (never their own experience), and they have a fear of the unknown (they cannot confidently explain how lucid dreaming occurs) so they deem the experience to be unnatural and connected to the paranormal.

I have done extensive research into lucid dreaming, as well as reflecting on my own experiences and the experiences of others, and I have discovered no conclusive reports or scientific/medical proof that lucid dreaming causes mental health deterioration. Nor do I believe it has any type of connection

with the spirit realm because you do not encounter spiritual entities or use your higher self in a lucid dreaming episode. It is your imagination and conscious awareness that allows you to lucid dream. The only possible downfall to lucid dreaming I have found is the potential to feel tired and unrested upon awakening. I can only speculate why this could occur, and I feel it could be to do with our conscious awareness and imagination being more active in a lucid dreaming state.

Time to lucid dream!

Now that you are intrigued by the fascinating phenomenon of lucid dreaming, your next questions will most likely be: how do I begin? Or, what do I need to do? There are extensive online sources, books, and seminars that can provide numerous in-depth techniques, tips, and advice on how to lucid dream. For me, however, I like to keep things as simple as possible because I find the less complicated and easy something is to follow (especially when you are learning), the more likely you are to resonate with the steps being offered and stay committed to practising.

Here are the five essential steps for lucid dreaming.

1) **Awake test:**

    Throughout the day, repeatedly ask yourself if you are dreaming, and perform an 'awake test' by using an object, physical movement/hand gesture (e.g., pinching your nose, wiggling your toes, clapping your hands in a certain way, whistling, snapping your fingers), or looking at the time on a clock. (Think of Leonardo DiCaprio's character in the movie *Inception*, and how he uses the spinning object to check whether he is dreaming or awake in the physical world.)

This first step is important because our subconscious mind registers and holds on to our habits, routines, and repetitive thought patterns. So, if you begin asking yourself whether you are dreaming (or perform a specific physical gesture) several times a day consecutively for a month, there is no doubt that your subconscious mind will register the repetitive thought pattern. You will soon begin asking yourself the same question in the dream realm, which can prompt a state of conscious awareness that you are, in fact, dreaming.

2) Mantra:

Repeat a specific mantra to yourself several times (for a couple of minutes) before you drift to sleep. Or introduce chanting the mantra into your evening meditation as this is a powerful way to set your intention in your subconscious mind. Possible mantras include:

I will realise I am dreaming.
I will wake up in my dream.
I will control my dreams.

3) Alarm:

Set your alarm to ring three to four hours after you go to sleep in the evening. If you are feeling extra enthusiastic, set your alarm to ring in the early morning (approximately one to two hours before you would normally wake up).

Allow yourself to be awakened by your alarm, keep yourself relaxed and your mind clear of any thoughts, repeat your mantra (from Step 2) to yourself for a couple of minutes, and then let yourself drift back to sleep. Training your

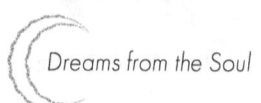

mind to stay 'consciously aware' while your body slips back into sleep is a wonderful way to help induce lucid dreaming.

When you are awakened by your alarm during the night or in the early hours of the morning, unless you are going to write down a dream in your journal *do not* check your phone or go to the kitchen for a snack, otherwise your mind will begin to disconnect from its restful and altered state.

4) Dream journaling:

Start writing down your dreams in a journal. Regardless of whether you feel the details from your dreams are unimportant, strange, or scattered, ensure you write them down or record yourself speaking.

When you start writing down your dream experiences, you become increasingly connected to your psyche, intuition, and collective consciousness. This is essential for lucid dreaming or any type of dream work you may be doing.

5) The three Ps:

Practice, patience, and persistence.

To develop your ability to induce lucid dreaming, you need to practise consistently, be persistent with the steps you choose to follow, and, most importantly, have patience!

Lucid dreaming experiences

Below is a lucid dreaming account shared by a female in her early twenties, who experiences lucid dreaming on a regular basis. She wanted to share what lucid dreaming feels like to her and what she experiences when it occurs.

I want to make it known that I don't go out of my way to try and lucid dream, it's just something that will naturally happen and at seemingly random times. I'm never in a deep sleep when I'm lucid dreaming and can still hear background noises from the physical world, such as traffic noises, dogs barking, and people talking.

Generally, when I lucid dream the scenario will be a situation I want to leave or change, such as being chased by something/someone, or I need to save a lot of people in the dream from a threat of some kind. It's like I take on the role of a protector. A thought will come into my head, telling me that 'I need to go up into the sky.' It's strange because the exact moment I hear this thought, I automatically realise that I can control myself, my actions, and act on my own accord. When I travel up into the sky, I'll always transform into something else and rarely stay in my human form. Usually, I'll transition into a dragon, or, if I remain as myself, I'll be able to fly or have other super abilities.

When I lucid dream, it always feels like I have a goal to complete, and I need to protect the other dream characters from whatever the threat may be. Once I complete this task, I find that I can change my dream however I please; like the scenery and what I'm doing. Lucid dreaming for me seems to connect with the concept of a game, because before I can move forward and have freewill, I must bypass the obstacles and reach the next level. Also, it's amazing when I lucid dream as my view of the dream scene will change perspectives – I can see what's happening from a first- and third-person perspective.

The second lucid dreaming experience I would like to share is my own. Shortly before I began writing this book, I developed a keen interest in lucid dreaming and started practising (using the simple steps I mentioned earlier), and after a few weeks I experienced my first lucid dream! I continued with my practice and soon regularly started having lucid dreams. If you follow the three Ps and the simple steps, I guarantee you will be lucid dreaming in no time!

My own lucid dreaming experience

It was around 7am when I awakened to the noise of my dogs barking and running around the house. But I was still tired and wanted to sleep for a little longer. Before I initially awoke, I was in the middle of a dream that I did not like, and I knew something bad was going to happen.

I continued to drift in and out of consciousness, despite hearing the commotion around me. Every time I fell back to sleep, I kept returning to the same dream and it would start from the exact same spot where I had awoken from it. However, when I entered the dream for the third or fourth time, I was suddenly able to use my voice in the dream and relay the words I wanted to. I began changing certain things about the dream because I subconsciously knew I had the ability to do so. As I was beginning to change more elements in the dream, I was unfortunately startled awake by my dog jumping on me!

Note: my first lucid dream is undoubtedly small and uneventful when compared to other lucid dreaming experiences, where the individual can dramatically alter and change nearly every aspect of their dreams. Nonetheless, I was over the moon and thought it was an amazing experience, and it prompted me to explore lucid dreaming more deeply as a regular practice.

The lucid dreaming experiences I encounter most often nowadays – since I no longer actively try to induce lucid dreams (I am currently using my dreams for spiritual and personal growth) – is the ability to control what I say in the dream realm, and if I am angry at a dream character then I can control my actions to hit them or fight back. I have also noticed that when I am experiencing a lot of stress, pressure to keep up with my study and work, and mentally and physically I am feeling burnt out, it will often trigger me to lucid dream.

In my lucid dreams, I will let all the stress, built-up emotions, and conflicted thoughts completely overtake me, as I yell and fight the targeted dream characters who cross my path. Quite often, when I awaken from an unintentional lucid dreaming experience, I cannot help but be shocked and laugh at what I said or did!

CHAPTER 13

The Falling Sensation

I choose to hold you in my dreams,
For in my dreams, you have no end.
~ Rumi

The Falling Sensation

Imagine lying in your bed in a relaxed, drowsy, and peaceful state of mind. Then suddenly you feel a strong, unexpected jolt travel through your entire body, which causes you to disconnect from your tranquil state and triggers the automatic urge to sit, stand-up, or hold on to the surface below you!

The falling sensation (also known as a hypnic jerk) is an unusual and startling experience that most commonly occurs when an individual is resting, sleeping, meditating, or astral projecting. As you may have already guessed from the title, the reason this peculiar sensation is called 'falling' is due to the overwhelming feeling that your physical body has begun to free-fall from an unseen height. Because this sensation is most frequently experienced when an individual has entered or is on the cusp of entering an altered state of consciousness, our subconscious mind and instinctual response is promptly activated to help alert and awaken us.

Scientific studies and research surmise that the unintentional sensation of falling, and the subconscious bodily response to jerk our body awake, is due to an overstimulated mind, anxiety, stress, or too much caffeine. Now, I do not doubt and cannot dispute that an individual who has an overactive mind, high stress levels, or caffeine overload will encounter great difficulty when trying to relax, switch-off, and unwind from distractions in the evening.

What I find most interesting, however, is that everyone I have discussed this unusual phenomenon with and surveyed in online questionnaires, reports *not* experiencing the falling sensation when they have been stressed, anxious or worried, or have consumed too much caffeine, sugar, or a large meal before bed (which are believed to be the underlying triggers). Instead, they report experiencing symptoms such as restlessness, an inability to get comfy (tossing and turning in bed), struggling to sleep, or sleeping lightly and awakening often, and racing thoughts and agitation.

What I discovered and found fascinating is that most people recall experiencing the falling sensation when they are about to drift to sleep, are in an extremely relaxed state, have just begun dreaming, are entering the astral realm, or are meditating. However, I do not claim to be right or disagree with the scientific theory about this peculiar sensation. Just like with everything written in this book, I simply aspire to share my views that are derived from a spiritual and intuitive frame of mind, and the opinions and experiences others have shared with me.

I hope to open your eyes to other possibilities and perspectives too…

My understanding of the falling sensation

For those who astral travel, undergo vision quests, or try to spiritually ascend during meditation, every time you involve yourself in these practices you are temporarily projecting a part of yourself into the universe. Some may deem this part to be the soul, collective consciousness, psyche, universal energy, etheric vessel, or spiritual body.

Despite the majority of the spiritual, dream, and out-of-body experiences we undertake being positive, empowering, and eye-opening in many ways, and just as danger exists in our physical world, there is potential harm that exists in the spirit world. This threat may be darker spiritual forces and energies that do not have our best interest at heart, or entities that carry unfinished business from their previous life. If we were to encounter such negativity in our altered state of consciousness, our instincts and intuition would trigger us to retreat from the potential danger. This is when the free-falling sensation is experienced and we are abruptly jerked from our relaxed trance state, and the part of ourselves that was projected outwards is returned safely to our body.

But perhaps it does not even need to be a negative spiritual experience that triggers the falling sensation. If you are anything like me and believe in divine timing (the universe aligns certain events to occur at a specific moment in our life), then I wonder whether when we enter a relaxed and intuitive state our higher self and collective consciousness may unintentionally ascend too deeply. We may be on the cusp of experiencing visions we are not yet ready to receive, precognitive knowledge about life situations, meeting our power animal or spirit guides before we are ready to do so, or recalling memories from our past lives that are too intense or painful for us to process. In other words, the falling sensation may be a protective response from our higher self, to help us remain safe, grounded, and connected to the present moment.

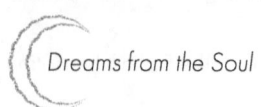

Personal experience

The reason I originally became interested in the falling sensation was because nearly every time I astral projected or meditated, I would experience the unusual free-falling feeling. It never occurred when I was deeply sleeping or lightly dozing, only when I was involved in a spiritual/meditative practice. I would feel a powerful shock course through my body and then the feeling of falling at an extremely fast pace. This caused me to abruptly awaken, and then my body would hit and bounce back against the surface I was lying on. This experience occurred specifically when I felt my body and mind slipping into a deeper spiritual state.

CHAPTER 14

Sleep Paralysis

For often, when one is asleep, there is something in consciousness which declares that what then presents itself is but a dream.
~ Aristotle

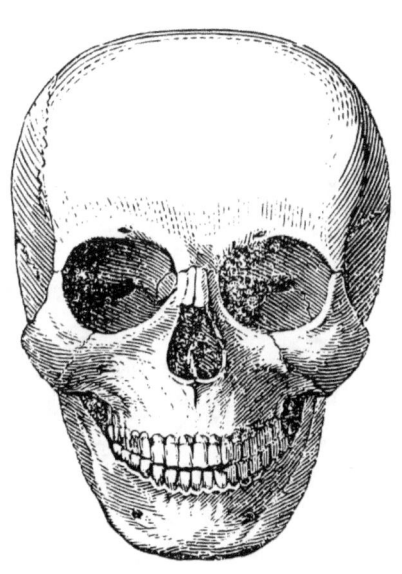

Sleep Paralysis

Have you ever experienced the sensation of being physically and verbally paralysed when you begin awakening from a dream or just before you fall asleep? The inability to thrash around and move your body or call out for help using your voice are seemingly impossible tasks when someone is experiencing sleep paralysis. Naturally, when we are inhibited from performing a simple task, like moving our body at will, it is an unsettling experience. Now, imagine feeling like 'something' is watching, waiting, or growling at you while you are paralysed! It is no wonder sleep paralysis can prove to be a tremendously frightening and mentally distressing experience.

Sleep paralysis is an enthralling concept to me, due to the underlying supernatural element involved with the experience. Looking at the history of sleep paralysis, there are dozens of varying cultural legends involving malevolent supernatural creatures of the night. You only need to read/listen to the real-life accounts people have shared about their sleep paralysis episodes to notice the underlying pattern of supernatural factors being mentioned in the experiences.

People frequently recall seeing spiritual or demonic beings, distorted shapes and bodies, the sound of growling, whispering, or as though fingernails are being dragged across a hard surface, and dark shadows appearing randomly around the room. The overwhelming feeling of 'fear and threat' from an unseen, unknown, and unexplainable source is a collective opinion shared by those who have experienced sleep paralysis.

Common themes associated with sleep paralysis:

* Being strangled (struggling to breathe, shortness of breath, inability to speak aloud).
* Sexual assault.
* Heavy pressure felt on chest (the feeling of someone sitting or pressing down on your chest).
* The sounds of loud growling, scratching, whispering, or hearing another language being spoken.
* Physically being grabbed by the legs, arms, torso, neck, hair, etc.
* Footsteps or the sound of something scampering up the walls/along the ground.
* Seeing demonic figures and disfigured spiritual entities.
* The feelings of terror, anxiousness, extreme fear, and desperation to escape or hide.
* Shadows appearing around the room that are unexplainable.

Do legends hold the answer to sleep paralysis?

Various cultures, tribes, and spiritual and religious belief systems have stories or legends about shadow beings, night-crawlers, and dark spiritual entities that prey upon victims when they are in a vulnerable state of consciousness (sleeping), and suffering with a physical or mental illness.

In Christian religion and demonology, one of the most well-known supernatural entities that is associated with sleep paralysis attacks are the 'succubi and incubi'. These demonic entities possess the ability to shapeshift into captivatingly attractive males and females. They are believed to visit people while they are asleep or they create an episode of sleep paralysis to ensure they have full control over their chosen victims, and then proceed to assault them physically or sexually. In certain cases, the individual who experiences a sleep paralysis attack will reveal that they initially enjoyed the sexual experience (they report seeing a beautiful female/male and believe it is their own sexual desires or fantasies that are causing the episode), up until the moment the demon reveals its true form.

There are an astounding number of variations of the incubi myth all around the world.

According to the legends, the succubus is defined as the female counterpart to the incubus, which is male. However, there are numerous stories and opinions that believe there is only one true demon (an incubus), and that it can shapeshift into both the male and female form. There are an astounding number of variations of the incubi (creatures of the night) myth all around the world, and they always link back to the underlying elements of fear, paralysis, horror, and physical and sexual violence.

A fascinating fact is the similar details shared between those who report being abducted by aliens in their bed and those who experience sleep paralysis. Unfortunately, due to the strong potential of encountering ridicule and judgement from others, many people keep their supernatural (often frightening) experiences to themselves and feel alone with what they are going through.

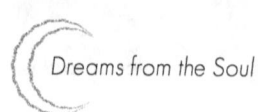

Dreams from the Soul

Mixed signals or spiritual experience?

Many argue that whatever is seen, felt, smelt, or heard during a sleep paralysis episode is merely an imaginative visual projection, created by the mind in a similar way to when we dream of themes, archetypes, and metaphors. Because sleep paralysis occurs when the body's nervous system is in a parasympathetic state and the mind is drowsy, it is fair to argue that the brain could accidentally send mixed signals to the conscious/subconscious mind. This may spark confusion as to whether the individual is awake, asleep, or dreaming, which could trigger the manifestation of peculiar sensory hallucinations. However, this is just a working theory that has yet to be definitively proven.

So, while there is no conclusive answer regarding what causes sleep paralysis (physiological or supernatural component), two questions remain firmly in the back of my mind:

* Why would someone who does not believe in paranormal and spiritual phenomena 'imagine or hallucinate' a terrifying spiritual presence during their sleep paralysis episode?
* Why are sleep paralysis experiences always associated with evil, demonic beings, fear, and violence?

Sleep paralysis experiences

This chapter would not be complete unless I included real-life sleep paralysis accounts!

Experience one

I was awoken by two dark shadows standing either side of my bed. They had almost like a smoky haze that was surrounding them. They started shaking my bed violently and I was screaming that I didn't want to go with them, and for them to stop shaking the bed. I kept screaming and was unable to move my body. I managed to get myself out of the frozen state by shouting several times, but I don't know whether I shouted aloud or in my head. I didn't want to go back to sleep that night. I was terrified.

Note: the individual who experienced this sleep paralysis episode had a daughter who was trying to astral project and was deeply into spirituality at the time. She told her daughter to stop astral projecting because she felt the dark spiritual entities were a result of her opening the 'astral/spiritual' realm with her practices. Her daughter ceased astral projecting immediately and the mother has never experienced sleep paralysis again.

This is a perfect example of delving into the spiritual/astral realms and experiencing a supernatural attack as a result. Although the sleep paralysis episode did not affect the daughter specifically, we may find that her mother did not have strong mental or spiritual blocks in place to deflect lower-vibrating spiritual energies; unlike her daughter, who was able to deflect unwanted spiritual energies/beings during her astral projection episodes. Remember, when we become curious and involved in a world that is not our own, the other world becomes curious in us.

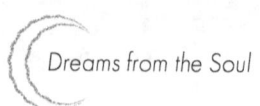

Experience two

It was mid-afternoon by the time I'd finally finished and submitted every assignment that was due for university. I was really exhausted and drained both physically and mentally. I was only having a couple hours' sleep each night because I had so much work to do and was practically a walking zombie.

I laid down on my bed and within moments I was asleep. Upon waking, I thought I had been asleep for hours, but when I tried to turn my head and look at my phone for the time, I realised I couldn't move any part of my body. I could hear the voices of my family in the background as they walked through the house, and I started yelling out for them to help me. It was in that moment that I suddenly realised the shadows of long clawed hands were reaching across my bedroom towards me. I was hysterical and kept trying to wake myself up because the hands were moving further towards me, and I could hear a distant growling sound. The growling was downright petrifying, and I just kept yelling, and finally managed to move my body and jolted awake. I looked at my phone and noticed I'd only been asleep for a few minutes. When I asked my family if they heard me screaming for help, they said no.

Sleep paralysis, in my eyes, clearly demonstrates how only a thin veil separates us from the spirit world, and all it takes is for us to slip into an altered state of consciousness to access it.

Did you know...

* Some individuals will experience sleep paralysis nearly every time they try to awaken from their dreams! I once knew a woman who had to deal with sleep paralysis several times a week, for a few months in a row, until it began to subside. She had no underlying mental or physical health issues, or difficult life situations to potentially explain why she was experiencing repetitive sleep paralysis episodes.
* Sleep paralysis sufferers have the potential to develop an unbalanced emotional and mental state, due to the dread and fear they carry in their psyche from their spiritual attack.
* During a sleep paralysis episode, most people are consciously aware of their physical surrounds. They can see the layout of the room they are paralysed in, feel the temperature on their skin, smell any scents that are drifting through the air, and can hear the background voices and noises that are happening around them, such as people having a conversation in their house, the neighbour's dog barking across the street, or a loud truck driving by.

CHAPTER 15

Astral Projection

Dreams are the guardians of sleep and not its disturbers.
~ Sigmund Freud

Astral projection is an enthralling out-of-body experience (OBE) that involves reaching a significant state of relaxation, a shift of consciousness (altered state change), and the transition between the physical world to the astral world, through the projection of energy.

The core concept of astral projection is that we as human beings possess the ability to project our astral self away from our physical body, with the intention to freely explore the astral realms without anything holding us back. Like with dreaming, astral projection requires our predominant conscious state of mind to shift into an altered state, so our higher self, intuition, and spiritual energy can flow freely without interruption from our analytical and rational mind.

When discussing astral projection, I use the term 'astral self or astral body' rather than 'astral form', which is most often referred to in astral-related discussions. I feel that using the phrase 'form' is impersonal and creates a sense of disconnection between the relationship we share with our astral and physical body. The term 'self or body' reminds us that our soul, spirit, collective consciousness, and metaphysical and physical body are all interconnected with one another and create our authentic self.

Before we move ahead and explore astral projection in a deeper and more profound light, there are four frequently asked questions I would like to address. I have answered these

Dreams from the Soul

from an open-minded and spiritualist perspective, and through the various views, ideas, and experiences shared by others.

Question 1: What is the astral self/body?

This is not a question that can be answered with an abrupt and close-ended response. So, I have provided various views and opinions, which will help prompt you to formulate your own ideas about the answer. I will reiterate that it does not matter if you do not connect with any of the examples I have written, as that is not the purpose. The purpose is for you to become curious and increasingly more introspective.

Answer 1: There is no astral self

The astral self is purely a figment of the imagination or a myth we have been led to believe. Sceptics and non-believers of spirituality and universal realms deem astral projection as being an imaginary journey. The astral self is considered a foolish concept because humans cannot be anything beyond the physical body and brain. All self-proclaimed astral journey experiences are nothing more than a subconscious manifestation and an imaginative idea.

Although this may seem like a harsh and closed-minded viewpoint, it is a fair assumption for sceptics to make. The reason being, from early childhood our mind begins imagining and envisioning itself in the fairytales and magical lands from the books that are read to us. We then begin watching movies, creating games with our friends, playing on tablets and phones, and exploring the internet. We listen to song lyrics, daydream about scenarios in our head, cross paths with numerous people from diverse ethnic, religious, and spiritual backgrounds, and certain people will dabble in psychedelic/substance experiences. In other words, all the activities, outlets, and experiences I have just mentioned naturally expand our imagination and creative thinking, which would make it easy for our mind to draw upon this subconscious material to envision a detailed, imaginary 'astral' journey.

Answer 2: Auric energy/universal vibration

We all have our own unique auric energy and universal vibration. Automatically, you may assume this sounds like our 'soul or spiritual energy'; however, there are varying views and beliefs that argue our auric energy and universal vibration have nothing to do with a spiritual or soulful element and are separate things entirely. With this theory, it is believed that the unique energy and vibration we carry throughout our lives – which is constructed through our personality and life experiences and is not something we are born with/destined to have – is projected into the astral realm, and our soul and spiritual energy remain completely attached to us.

Regarding this theory, astral projection is not perceived as a spiritual experience because we are not using any element of the soul or spirit, but rather we are using our energy and vibration. When we enter a room full of people, we recognise their unique and individual vibration, just as they respond to ours on an intuitive level, and we naturally pick up on the collective energy of the environments we are in. The same concept is believed to occur using this astral projection theory: we mindfully project our energy and vibration into the astral realm and merge with the energy that resides within these realms.

Answer 3: Spiritual energy

In contrast to the prior answers, this viewpoint is formulated specifically through the lenses of spirituality, psyche, and soul. For spiritualists, the term 'astral self' is simply another phrase used to describe our spiritual body. Our spiritual body/energy/self (whichever term you prefer to use) is the collective essence of the universe, our soul, spirit, clair-senses, psyche, consciousness, and past lives. When we astral project, we are drawing upon our spiritual energy, utilising the power of our Third Eye to experience visions of the astral realm and are projecting a small part of our spiritual body into the astral realm. Thus, this theory deems our astral self and astral journey to be a spiritual experience, rather than being something that stems from the imagination or a separate part of ourselves. Just like when we meditate, experience precognitive or spiritual visions, and partake in spiritual practices, we channel and project a small part of our spiritual self/energy into our work, and astral projection is no different.

Question 2: What is the astral realm?

What do you think the astral realm is and how would you try to describe it? This is one of those questions where we need to step outside the box of physicality and methodical thinking. The 'astral realm' is a broad expression that encompasses varying metaphors, meanings, and underpinnings. First, we need to understand that the astral realm (or spirit realm for that matter) cannot be defined in a single-word answer, nor can it be concluded as something specific and definite. We cannot objectively simplify and label the mysterious, powerful, and infinite energy of the universe, spiritual and astral realms. There are 195 countries that exist on Earth and close to eight billion people. If we take into consideration how large our physical world is, can you imagine how limitless the astral/spiritual realm is?

The astral realm cannot be understood as a 'particular thing', such as a tropical island, a car, building, or flower. In our physical world, although we perceive and encounter life events, objects, and environments in different ways, ultimately, we all share a similar experience regarding what we witness, smell, touch, and hear. However, when it comes to the astral realm, our individual experiences will be extraordinarily different to one another, which consequently makes it difficult to define 'what' the astral realm essentially is and what someone will experience in their astral journey.

Astral realm experiences include:

* projecting to the higher or lower astral/spiritual planes
* encountering helpful or trickster astral/spiritual animals and beings
* having the ability to fly or float effortlessly in the astral realm
* struggling to project beyond the environments you know
* being able to visit cities and environments you have never physically been to
* having spiritual visions.

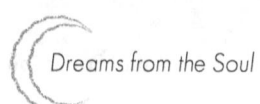

Question 3: Why astral project?

People most frequently astral project for the following reasons:

* Human curiosity!
* Desire to explore alternative astral planes and have an OBE without the need for hallucinogens.
* Seeking interaction or answers from spirit guides and other astral beings.
* Experiencing the ability to project your energy and fly, float, or swim without feeling the weight and restriction from your physical body.
* Interest in learning about the astral plane and what exists in it.
* Seeking proof that life beyond this world exists.
* Interest in developing a deeper connection with your astral self/body.

Question 4: Is astral projection safe?

Something that immediately stood out to me during my research of astral projection was the repetitive reassurance that astral projection is completely safe for 'everyone' with no potential risks involved. I strongly disagree with this opinion for three main reasons:

1) Any time spiritual practices, vision quests, astral journeying, and OBEs take place, there is an underlying risk of encountering low-vibrating and negative spiritual energies, beings, and visions. You also have the potential to become spiritually, mentally, or physically drained after

the experience because you are using your energy and clair-senses for your astral/spiritual practices.

2) You may experience a complication in reconnecting your astral self/body back to your physical body when you return from your astral journey. This problem will generally occur if you were to accidentally fall asleep during your astral journey, or if you are abruptly jolted out of your relaxed state before you can envision yourself reconnecting with your physical body. (I have personally encountered this complication once before, and I will share my experience later in the chapter.)

3) For people who have unstable mental health or underlying psychological issues, OBEs like astral projection can be extremely dangerous and potentially triggering. Astral projection – and many types of state-change practices – increase the risk of paranoia, psychosis, and anxiety-based thinking in those who have schizophrenia, bipolar disorder, PTSD, mania, depression, and anxiety.

After reading through the potential risks, I hope I have not scared you away! I just want to ensure that everyone who partakes in astral projection understands that it is not a joke, and proper methods need to be used to ensure you are safe during your astral journeying and when your spiritual/astral body returns (reconnects) with your physical body.

How to astral project

There are a vast number of techniques that are designed to help you project your astral self away from your physical body. I have chosen to focus on two that are the most widely recognised, and I have personally utilised myself and found effective.

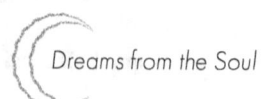

1) **Visualisation** (reflection off your physical appearance):

    Visualisation (also referred to as ghosting and reflection) is when you rely closely on visualising and your felt senses. As you descend into a deeper state of relaxation using your chosen meditative or state-change process, you begin to visualise your astral body (which reflects your physical appearance) slowly sitting up and rising gently from your physical body. As you continue visualising your astral body, concentrate on how your physical body seems to be increasingly lighter and more relaxed.

    Starting from your toes and travelling all the way up to the top of your head, notice how weightless you are becoming and allow your astral body to rise completely away from your physical body. Gradually, your astral body will hover/float above your physical body, and when the time feels right, give yourself the silent permission to float freely around the room, throughout your home, outside, and to the environments and places that are familiar to you.

2) **Climbing the rope/ladder:**

    Climbing a symbolic rope or ladder is a classic and popular technique that frequently appears in astral projection tutorials. Following the same process as above, once you have entered an adequate state of deep relaxation in your mind and physical body, instead of visualising a reflection of yourself, you are going to envision that there is either a rope or ladder hanging above your body. You cannot initially see the top of it because there is no end to the infinite astral realm.

    In your mind, begin climbing the rope/ladder, and when you feel instinctively ready to step away from it or let go, gently do so. Some people may notice that their rope/

ladder will abruptly end, or they will feel a strong urge to stop, and this simply means they have reached a place in the astral plane that their intuition and astral body feel comfortable to explore in that moment.

Important: as your astral body climbs the ladder or rope, do not rush this process as it represents the transition between the physical world and astral world.

Note: both techniques may take as little as 10 minutes to work for some people, and others may find the process will require up to 40 minutes. Everyone reaches a state of relaxation in their mind and body at a different pace, and this will influence the timing of their astral journey. Regardless of how long it takes you in the early stages of your practice, the more consistent and patient you are, the more quickly you will gain the ability to relax and visualise more clearly.

Astral projection tips

* *White light energy.* Pray or call upon the spiritual deities you believe in and ask them to place the white light of protection around your physical and astral body before you commence projecting. This protective and positive universal energy will help keep you safe from lower-vibrating and negative beings.
* *Relax.* Inducing an adequate state of relaxation before astral projecting is essential. Choose a form of meditation or breathwork ritual that works for you, and concentrate on creating a sense of stillness, peace, clarity, and calmness in your body and mind. Release all tension, stress, and wandering thoughts.

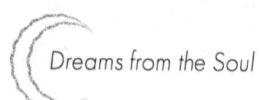

* *Mindfulness.* When you begin envisioning your astral body disconnecting from your physical body, and as you climb the metaphorical rope/ladder, ensure your mind is focused fully on this task. Do not try to imagine or think about the things you want to experience in the astral realm because this will create a false experience.

  You may find yourself struggling to see anything for the first several minutes in your astral journey (you may just see total darkness) and this is completely normal. You will soon begin to see glimpses of colours and shapes, and your vision of the astral realm will become increasingly clear.

* *Expectations.* Release any high expectations or preconceived ideas you may have about astral projection and the astral realm. Your experience will be different to others and to what you imagine. Go into astral projection with an open mind!

* *Instincts.* If at any point during your astral journey you begin to feel unsafe and your intuition is telling you that something does not feel right, leave the astral realm and reconnect with your physical body immediately. Do not ignore your instincts just to appease your curiosity.

* *Timing, distractions, and comfortability.* Astral projection can be done any time of the day, providing you can find a quiet environment to relax comfortably in, without any distractions. If you are someone who struggles to unwind or nap during the daytime, then you will find it more effective to astral project in the evening when you are naturally more relaxed. With astral projecting, traditionally you would lie flat on your back on a comfortable surface, such as a bed or lounge.

* *Familiarity.* Initially when people first begin astral projecting, they tend to explore familiar places and surroundings, such as their home or their friends/loved one's homes, the circuit they walk their dog on, a local park or café they visit often, or their place of work.

   In the early stages of your astral projection practice, by projecting to the places that are most familiar to you, this is the easiest and safest approach to help you gain confidence, develop your astral skills and abilities, and acquaint yourself with the energy of the astral plane. Once you cover the basics and begin developing your astral journeying skills, you can then start envisioning yourself climbing the rope/ladder higher into the astral plane – this is when your experiences in the astral realm will become more vivid, unusual, and symbolic.

   In my mind, and although it may be completely different to others, I have always found that the higher I climb the rope/ladder with my astral self, the more deeply I step into the astral/spiritual realm.

Personal experience

As mentioned earlier, I once encountered a problem during an astral projection experience. Prior to this event, I had only experienced positive astral projection journeys. One evening, I decided to astral project before going to sleep, as I normally did. I always used the 'climbing the rope' technique and soon found myself drifting into deep relaxation and an altered-state change. The astral journey began like normal as I floated out of my home and neighbourhood. However, during some point in my astral journey I unintentionally fell asleep. I did not visualise my astral body reconnecting with my physical body, and this triggered a tangible change in the energy dynamic of the astral realm.

I experienced what I can only describe as a strange sort of 'limbo' between the dream and astral realm. I could no longer control my actions completely and began to feel a dark and ominous presence around me. My vision abruptly shifted, and I started seeing a terrifying, large, horned spiritual entity. The vision kept changing until I was suddenly back at home with my family, and the entity was chasing and torturing my family. This terrible vision lasted for the entire night, and I could not wake myself up regardless of what I tried. I could not control anything that was happening, and I was forced to watch the horned entity.

It was my alarm in the morning that finally woke me up and removed me from the shocking vision. I tried to push aside what I had seen and went about my day, but the next night I had a similar violent vision of the entity again in my dreams. I did not tell anyone in my family what I was experiencing, but when I arrived back from work the following evening, my sister said she felt like something was watching her during the day. She had seen a silhouette of a horned man standing in her bedroom doorway.

I completely freaked out at this point because there was no way she could have known about my visions or the horned entity! I then told my family about what I had seen during my astral journey and dream visions. For the following several days, I continually saw a dark, horned silhouette in the corner of my eye, and when I left for work in the mornings and reversed out the driveway, I saw the entity standing in the window of our spare room (as it always did in my visions). I was experiencing spiritual dream attacks every night and the violence and fear kept getting worse.

Eventually, after two weeks, my mother was able to cleanse and clear the house of the horned spiritual entity. My spiritual attacks ceased, my dreams returned to normal, and the horned entity was not seen again by any of us. Consequently, after this negative experience and the deep-rooted fear it invoked in me, I avoided astral projecting for over two years. I have never since experienced anything negative, frightening, or threatening in my astral journeys and now enjoy regularly delving into the astral realm!

CHAPTER 16

Tools for Dream Work

The interpretation of dreams is the royal road to a knowledge of the unconscious activities of the mind.
~ SIGMUND FREUD

- *I cannot remember my dreams!*
- *How can I begin interpreting the meaning of my dreams if I cannot clearly recall everything?*
- *The details I write down from my dreams are random, unhelpful, or simply do not make sense!*

By far, the most common question I am asked by people is, 'How can I remember my dreams?' This is a fair and crucial question to ask because any dream interpretation requires content to work from. Up until 2017, when I was 21 years old, I had never written a dream down in my life, nor could I ever recall them, and did not have an interest in doing so because I did not see any point or value in it! However, when I first started experiencing journey dreams where my spirit animal began coming to me, I actively started trying to remember my dreams and journal them. It was as though a lightbulb had gone off in my mind, and I suddenly understood that dreams carry profound insight, answers, guidance, and opportunities for personal and spiritual growth.

> *Learning how to remember your dreams does not have to be a difficult, confusing, or costly process.*

Numerous dream techniques are advertised and portrayed in such a way that you *must* follow them, right down to the smallest detail, if you want to improve your dream memory recall. I am going to tell you right now: learning how to remember your dreams does not have to be a difficult, confusing, or costly process! Below, we will explore four simple steps that worked for me at the beginning of my dream journey, and which have worked for the countless people I have shared this advice with.

Four steps to remembering your dreams

1. Meditation

It seems that whenever you mention the word 'meditation' people audibly or internally sigh and roll their eyes. If this is you, and before you skip ahead to the next step, just take a moment to read why meditation is a wonderful practice for dream work and interpretation.

Cast aside any preconceived notion that meditation is only relevant to gurus or for gaining spiritual enlightenment. Meditation is a beautiful and powerful practice that assists in alleviating overthinking, decreasing pessimistic attitudes, and helping release stagnant energy and blockages from within our collective consciousness and wellbeing. It also helps us connect more deeply with our higher self and psyche (internal world), which strengthens our ability to recognise and understand ourselves, our dreams, and the worlds around us.

Meditation can be used in the following two ways for dream work.

Before-dream meditation

You can use meditation as a ritual to clear your mind and set your intention.

Many of us lead busy lives and do not have much energy by the end of the day. The thought of trying to stay awake and meditate before going to sleep can often seem like a daunting task! So, let us keep it simple and choose just 10 minutes for our evening meditation.

You could sit in a comfortable chair or lie on your bed during your meditation sessions. There is no right or wrong way, just do what feels right for you and will allow your body to relax completely for several minutes. Ensure no distractions are present, such as pinging phones, because this is going to disturb and ruin your meditative practice.

For the first few minutes, as you sit or lie comfortably, just focus on your breathing. Do not try to control your breathing, simply notice the rise and fall of your chest, and the gentle inhalation and exhalation of your breath. Your body may be restless and fidgety, and many thoughts may start flowing through your mind. Try not to control or force your body to remain still, but instead move the part that feels restless; for example, give your legs or arms a shake to loosen the built-up energy that is residing there. With your thoughts, let them pass through your mind freely without stopping them, but be mindful not to delve into them; for example, imagine your thoughts are the waves of the ocean and you are standing on the shore watching them roll in. You do not need to enter the water, but instead you can observe from afar.

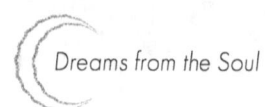

After a few minutes, you will notice that your mind has suddenly become quiet, your breathing slower, and your body is relaxed. This is when you are going to begin repeating to yourself, either aloud or within your mind:

I will remember my dreams.

Repeat this simple mantra to yourself several times, and when you feel you have said it enough, then you can allow yourself to drift off to sleep for the night.

Note: you may also use this 'repeating mantra' meditation technique if you have any question that you are seeking insight into. Instead of repeating to yourself that you will remember your dreams, repeat the question you want your higher self or spirit guides to answer in the dream realm. For example, 'Should I take the job promotion being offered to me?' Keep asking yourself the same question every night during meditation until you receive the guidance you are looking for in the dream realm.

It may take one night, several nights, or a couple of weeks before you receive an answer. Make sure you consistently write down every detail you can recall from your dreams because there may be an overlap in symbols or dream themes that will provide a clue or the answer to your query.

After-dream meditation

Focus on the concept of reflection and revelation.

You can use meditation to reflect on your dreams, discover their true meaning, and how they are relevant to your past, present, or future. This technique can be done in one of two ways, but it is most effective upon first awakening from a dream session.

When you first awaken is when the details of your dream are the clearest in your mind. It is essential to use this short window of time (within the first five minutes of waking up) to write down everything you can recall. Once you do this, you are then going to either close your eyes and concentrate on the memory of your dream or read the words/observe the sketches you have recorded in your dream journal.

For several minutes, reflect deeply on your dream. You may notice yourself unconsciously recalling more details from your dream, you might feel the need to write down (or draw) something, certain emotions may begin surfacing, or intuitively you might start making connections between the elements in your dream and a situation you are dealing with in waking life. Anything can come to you during after-dream meditation and it can prove extremely valuable in the interpretation process. The more you practise being present in the moment with your dream, the deeper intuitive reflections you will make, and the stronger your connection will become to your higher self and the language of your dreams.

If you are unable to meditate immediately upon awakening, then ensure you write down (or draw) everything you can recall from your dream, and then reflect on these details when you next meditate. Many people find it difficult to reconnect with their dreams after several hours or a couple of days, so please try to meditate as soon as possible so the dream is still clear and vivid in your mind. Otherwise, simply stick with meditating before you go to sleep.

Dreams from the Soul

2. Dream journaling

Journaling your dreams is essential for developing your ability to recall, decipher, and recognise recurring archetypes and symbols in your dreams.

When you awaken from sleeping, you usually only have a couple of minutes to vividly recall any key details, themes, thoughts, or reactions from your dreams. It is imperative during this short period of time that you quickly write down everything you remember about your dreams, without analysing or rationalising the details. Be careful not to fall into the habit of trying to decipher your dream as you are writing it down because this will prompt your logical and conscious mind to override your intuitive ability to recall key information.

Writing down your dreams in a journal prompts your subconscious mind to remember them. Just like with any habit and routine, the more we reinforce in our mind that we 'will remember and write down our dreams every night', it soon becomes second nature to us. Do not dismiss the power of subconscious reiteration and dream journaling because collectively they are the most powerful methods used in dream work for both beginners and those who can fluently recall their dreams.

Dreams are your personal and sacred connection to your psyche, the universe, and the spirit world, and you should honour this with a beautiful journal.

From 2017, when I first began writing down my dreams, until now, I have filled seven journals from front to back.

There will be days – and I even encountered six consecutive weeks – where I could not remember any of my dreams. Do not worry if this happens to you and, most importantly, do not make yourself feel bad that you seem to be unsuccessful in recalling your dreams. Often, when we are experiencing high stress, burnout, lack of adequate sleep, inconsistent sleep patterns, and when our mind is overflowing with thoughts, it can block us from remembering our dreams and connecting with our higher self. Rest assured this 'block' will pass, and you will suddenly find yourself recalling your dreams again.

Dream journals may be written in sentences, dot points, words scattered all over the page or using sketches; it ultimately comes down to what you feel comfortable doing. For certain people it may be easier and quicker for them to 'draw' what they recall from their dreams, rather than trying to write long sentences when they have just woken up. For those with no artistic ability, like myself, writing down the 'plot line' of the dream like a symbolic story is another approach. However, for the majority of us, it is common to write down disconnected and random words from our dreams, without clearly remembering the dream in great depth.

An example of disconnected words recalled from a dream could be:

Girl, train, horse riding, park, pink, long skirt.

I strongly guide you to dedicate a book solely to recording your dreams and do not use it for anything else (except if you are writing down messages or visions from your spirit guides). Dreams are your personal and sacred connection to your psyche, the universe, and the spirit world, and you should honour this with a beautiful journal. This does not mean your journal

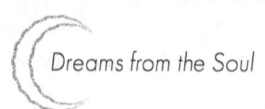
Dreams from the Soul

has to be expensive, a certain number of pages, or a specific colour; you simply need to choose a journal that you feel drawn to using for your dream work.

When you journal your dreams throughout the night or in the early hours, most of you will notice that your 'normally neat handwriting' becomes illegible! I personally use dream journals without ruled lines, or I simply ignore the lines and write freely all over the pages, while I am half-asleep. I have found that the more room I have on my page, the less likely I am to accidentally write over the same spot.

In your dream journal you may like to include the following points:

* The date the dream took place.
* The events, symbols, characters, scenery, and any details that you can recall.
* Your instinctive and intuitive reactions/feelings/thoughts that surface about your dream.
* What situations, obstacles, or stressors are occurring in your life when the dream took place. This will help you recognise whether your dream is connecting with a specific life event (past, present, or impending).
* Your personal interpretation of the dream. Intuitively writing down what you feel your dream is conveying to you.

3. Crystals for dream work

To enhance your dreaming experience, whether it is for the purpose of invoking lucid dreams, journey or sparked dreams, deeper and peaceful sleep, astral travel, spiritual growth, or psychic protection, you can always turn to Mother Earth's natural resources for a helping hand.

Crystals are a wonderful tool to implement into dream work and spiritual development. Crystals are not just beautiful to look at; they each have their own power and metaphysical energy that can be utilised to increase your connection to your psyche, spiritual nature, intuition, and dreams. My family's online holistic business is called MoonstoneGypsyAU, and my mama's mantra to all our wonderful customers for effectively using their crystals is:

Cleanse, charge, and program.

Cleanse and charge

Cleanse and charge your crystals before working with them so that the energy and intent is clear. Then, once you have finished using your crystals for dream, sleep, or spiritual work, ensure you cleanse them once again.

You can cleanse and charge your crystals using the following methods:

* Tibetan singing bowl
* White sage (smudging)
* Sunlight
* Element of water
* Moonlight (new moon and full moon lunar energy)
* Visualisation of white light energy
* Burying in the earth overnight

- Placing a clear quartz generator in the middle of the crystals you are going to work with, or placing your crystals on a selenite charging plate before use.

Program

It is vital to program a crystal before working with it, otherwise how will it know what to do for us? When you program your crystal, you are sharing your energy with it, establishing a connection with its ancient metaphysical properties, and setting your intention.

To program your crystals, try this effective method:

- Hold your crystal in your palms and place it in front of your Third Eye Chakra.
- With a relaxed and clear mind, speak aloud or silently to your crystals and tell them what you want them to do. For example: 'I need help remembering my dreams. I need help to lucid dream. I would like to sleep more deeply and restfully. I aspire to connect with my spirit guides in the dream realm. I wish for more vivid dreams. I want to have peaceful dreams and no nightmares.'
- Once you have programmed the crystals with your intent, ensure you pay your respects to the crystals.

The following crystals are perfect for sleep, psychic protection, OBEs (such as astral projection and vision quests), dream work and spiritual journeying.

Amethyst

- Gently and safely opens our Third Eye Chakra (spiritual eye).

Tools for Dream Work

- Promotes healing in the dream realm, for both our metaphysical and physical body.
- Wonderful for inducing journey dreams.
- Offers protection in OBEs, the dream realm, and during spiritual work.
- Helps us connect more deeply with our unconscious mind and spiritual nature.

Angelite

- Beautiful for connecting with spirit guides, angels, and deceased loved ones in the dream realm.
- Promotes peaceful and deep sleep.
- Provides reassuring and gentle dreams.
- Surrounds you in universal white light energy while you are in an altered state of consciousness.
- Gives a peaceful and serene energy that offers calming and peaceful dream experiences.
- A lovely crystal choice for children, older people, or for anyone who believes in a higher spiritual power.

Labradorite

- Enhances dream recall.
- Promotes vivid and sparked dreams.
- Strengthens our aura and balances our chakras.
- Offers protection within the dream realm.
- Repels unwanted spiritual energy away from you.
- Strengthens our psychic connection to our spirit guides. This is beneficial for anyone involved in spiritual

development/spiritual practices, and those who are seeking spiritual or precognitive dreaming experiences.

Lodalite, Herkimer diamond, and Moldavite

* Incredibly potent for astral projection and OBEs.
* Useful for lucid dreaming.
* Helps with spiritual ascension.
* Good for heightened and vivid dream experiences.
* Can be considered the powerhouse of crystals for OBEs, spiritual journeying, and dream work. They are high-vibration crystals that will induce intense dreaming and memorable astral experiences. However, these crystals are not recommended for beginners and should be used with caution and care. They should be avoided completely by older people and those suffering with mental health conditions.

Rainbow fluorite

* Enhances dream recall.
* Promotes clear and concise dreams.
* Brilliant for before- or after-dream meditation.
* Helps your mind retain important details from your dreaming experiences.
* Promotes clarity and clears distracting thoughts, which can potentially block your ability to have meaningful dreams or interpret them.

Rainbow moonstone

* Intuitive dreaming (connecting you with your higher self).

- Powerful for inducing journey, sparked, and past-life dreams.
- Brilliant for anyone who is contemplating significant life changes, feels stuck, aspires to find their purpose, and is looking for guidance in their dreams.
- When placed in your pillow or held during meditation, it will help connect you with your spirit guides, psychic abilities, and promote creative new ideas and self-realisations.

Rose quartz

- Encourages sweet dreams.
- Promotes peaceful and relaxing sleep.
- Perfect for those who experience nightmares and bad dreams.
- Sends gentle, loving, and nurturing energy to us in the dream realm.
- Connects with the Heart Chakra.
- Comforting crystal energy for young children and those who are emotionally sensitive.

Selenite

- Aligns you with the lunar energies and moon cycles.
- Peaceful sleep and chakra balancing.
- Gentle crystal energy for those who are seeking peaceful, relaxed, and non-vivid dreams.
- Selenite helps you raise your spiritual and cosmic vibration.
- If you aspire to astral travel or lucid dream, do so during the full moon with the help of selenite. Your intention will

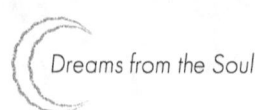

be amplified and the experience more potent because of the powerful lunar energy.

Smoky quartz

* Offers protection from spiritual and psychic attacks while dreaming and meditating.
* Helps to prevent sleep paralysis and nightmares.
* Grounding for your mindset, spiritual energy, and body (connects with the Root Chakra).
* Essential for anyone who experiences bad dreams or paranormal encounters. It is a highly protective crystal that will repel any negative and low-vibrating spiritual entities away from you, in both the physical world and in an altered state of consciousness.

To implement crystals into your dream, astral, and spiritual work, try using one or more of the following methods:

* Meditate while holding the crystal or placing it on your Third Eye Chakra. This is a wonderful spiritual and mindful practice.
* Place crystals in your pillow while you sleep. This is a simple and effective way to use crystals in dream work.
* Hold your crystals between your palms while astral projecting or position them around your body to form a protection circle.
* Place the crystals on your bedside table so their energy is close by you.
* Create a crystal grid dedicated to raising the spiritual vibration, dream experience, protection, and energy in your bedroom.

4. Essential natural herbs and oils

Essential herbs and oils have been used throughout history to heal physical ailments, elevate our mindset, relax our body, in conjure work, shamanic and spiritual rituals, and for enriching our wellbeing and our connection to the natural world.

Herbs and oils are brilliant to incorporate in your dream work. You can choose between drinking, smoking, or burning your chosen herbs, or placing a small satchel of herbs near your bed or in your pillow as you sleep. Otherwise, you may feel drawn to applying essential oil directly to your skin, ingesting in tincture form, placing droplets in an oil burner for aromatherapy, or applying a few droplets of oil on a piece of material and placing it under your pillow.

Important: please consult a medical professional prior to using any essential oils or herbs, especially if you have any underlying allergies, are pregnant or breastfeeding.

Below is a list of the most beneficial essential oils and herbs that are wonderful for dream work, sleeping, and spiritual development. Two fantastic herbs that I regularly use for dream and spiritual work are mugwort and valerian root.

Mugwort (*Artemisia vulgaris*) is used for:

* astral travel and OBEs
* inducing lucid dreaming
* vivid and intense dreams
* enhancing dream recall.

Mugwort has been used for centuries for prophecy, dream travel, and enhancing spiritual powers. It helps to naturally break down any psychic blocks within your consciousness that

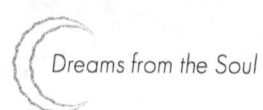

are preventing you from connecting with your imagination, psyche, and spiritual nature.

Mugwort is undoubtedly my absolute go-to herb for any dream work I am doing. It has an earthy and bitter flavour when consumed as a tea, so for those with a sweet tooth you may like to add a dash of honey, maple syrup or lemon balm.

Mugwort can be smoked, consumed as a tea, ingested through a tincture, applied as an essential roll-on oil, burnt as a smudge stick, or in loose leaf form.

Valerian root (*Valeriana officinalis*) is used for:

- deeper sleep
- decreasing anxiety and stress
- awakening dreams
- dream recall.

Valerian root is a well-known herb that has a natural sedative effect on the body and mind, which allows for deeper and more restful sleep to take place. It helps relieve anxiety, overthinking, and mental burden. Valerian root strengthens our ability to observe and recall our dreams in greater depth and clarity.

Valerian root can be consumed as a tea, in tincture and capsule form, or used as loose herbs to create a satchel that is placed near your sleeping space.

Additional natural herbs and essential oils that will positively assist you in your dream work journey include:

- Blue lotus
- Chamomile

- Frankincense
- Lavender
- Lemon balm
- Mexican dream herb
- Passionflower
- Patchouli
- Rose petals
- Skullcap
- Sun opener

Blue lotus (*Nymphea Caerulea*) is used for:

- psychic development
- enhanced meditative visions
- vivid dreams (often with an underlying spiritual element)
- mild aphrodisiac.

Blue lotus is a beautiful flower that offers multiple benefits ranging from enhanced spiritual visions, creative ideas, and vivid dreams, and is also recognised as a natural remedy for menstrual cramps.

Blue lotus can be consumed as tea (I recommend adding a spoonful of honey for sweetness as blue lotus tends to be bitter in taste), vaped, smoked, or inhaled through essential oil form.

Chamomile is used for:

- reducing feelings of anxiety and stress
- a natural relaxant for the body and mind
- helping induce positive dreams and deeper sleep.

Chamomile is a wonderful herb for those who experience nightmares, negative dreams, and suffer with anxiety.

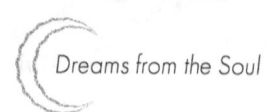

Chamomile helps to relax the body, soothe digestive issues, and promotes peaceful and calmer sleep.

Chamomile can be consumed as a tea, in tincture form, applied topically to the body, inhaled through essential oil, and used as loose herbs to create a satchel that is placed near your sleeping space or under your pillow.

Frankincense is used for:

* naturally grounding the body, mind, and spirit
* aiding in meditation
* promoting relaxation
* having clearer and more memorable dreams.

Frankincense naturally calms the body, slows down breathing, and is beneficial to use before meditation, astral projection, and sleep. Frankincense helps to open your higher chakras, connect more deeply with your spiritual energy, and increases dream activity.

Frankincense can be used in the form of essential oil, incense, and applied topically to the body.

Lavender is used for:

* a natural sedative for the body, mind, and senses
* promoting feelings of relaxation and calmness
* decreasing anxiety, worries, and stress
* peaceful sleep.

Lavender is a popular herb that is widely recognised for its beautiful scent and relaxing proprieties. Lavender assists in creating a tranquil state of mind, so that positive and peaceful dreams can take place during the night.

Lavender herb can be consumed as tea, applied topically to the body, inhaled through essential oil, air diffusers, or incense, and used as loose herbs to create a satchel that is placed near your sleeping space or under your pillow.

Lemon balm is used for:

- promoting deeper sleep
- enhancing dreams and dream recall
- those who suffer with depression, anxiety, and struggle to find calmness from within.

Lemon balm helps to boost the mindset in a positive and clear-thinking way. Lemon balm has been used throughout history to invoke a sense of balance and relaxation within the body, mind, and spirit, and assists in creating deeper sleeping episodes.

Lemon balm can be consumed as a tea, in tincture form, inhaled through essential oil, applied topically to the body, used as loose herbs to create a satchel that is placed near your sleeping space or under your pillow.

Mexican dream herb (*Calea zacatechichi*) is used for:

- increasing the number of dreams throughout the night
- vivid and longer dream episodes
- aiding in lucid dreaming.

Mexican dream herb is believed to assist in triggering precognitive dreams and memorable vivid dream episodes. Mexican dream herb is wonderful for anyone wanting to delve more deeply into dream work or who struggles to remember their dreams.

Mexican dream herb can be consumed as a tea (you can add a spoonful of honey or other herbs including chamomile or lemon balm to counteract the natural bitter taste of Mexican dream herb), smoked, capsule form, or applied topically to the body (temples and soles of feet).

Passionflower is used for:

* having vivid and colourful dreams
* a deeper relaxation and calmness within mind and body
* lucid dreaming.

Passionflower has gentle healing properties that create feelings of peacefulness and tranquility. The perfect herb to include in any dream work as it helps to induce brighter and more vivid dreams, which have a stronger opportunity to remain in the dreamer's mind upon awakening.

Passionflower can be consumed as a tea, in tincture, and capsule form.

Patchouli is used for:

* aiding in relaxation and releasing stress and tension from the body
* deeper meditation and spiritual vision experiences
* dispelling negative dreams
* balancing emotions and releasing stagnant energy from the metaphysical body.

Patchouli helps to strengthen your connection to the spirit world and your higher self. It is naturally calming for your emotions and invokes feelings of nostalgia, clarity, and relaxation.

Patchouli can be used by inhaling essential oil, air diffusers, or incense, and applied topically to the body.

Skullcap is used for:

* assisting in astral projection
* promoting feelings of calmness in the nervous system
* helping to relieve insomnia
* clearing the mind of thoughts.

Skullcap helps to reduce stress, busy minds, and naturally calms the body's nervous system. A wonderful herb choice for anyone who struggles to relax, experiences anxiety, and finds it difficult to initially fall asleep in the evening.

Skullcap can be consumed as a tea, in tincture form, and smoked.

Sun opener (*Heimia salicifolia*) is used for:

* opening your higher self to recall past-life memories and glimpses of future events
* enhancing meditation
* feelings of calmness and deep relaxation in mind and body
* aiding in lucid dreaming and astral projection.

Sun opener herb is believed to carry ancient metaphysical properties that allow for spiritual ascension, clearer and vivid visions, and clears the mind of thoughts to allow intuitive wisdom to flow through more freely.

Sun opener herb can be consumed as a tea, smoked, and in tincture form.

These herbs can help you with: relieving stress, anxiety, and insomnia; naturally relaxing the body and mind; slowing down your heart rate and blood pressure; promoting peaceful dreams; inducing blissful or intense meditation sessions; having profound spiritual and dream visions; having soulful revelations and sparked dreams; having a heightened awareness and lucid ability in the dream realm; triggering OBEs; attaining deeper sleep; and having less sporadic waking up during the night.

Note: if you use essential oils for your dream work or aspire to experience peaceful dreams and less restlessness in the evening, then placing a few droplets in your bath or massaging the oil into the soles of your feet, temples, or wrists are easy ways to enjoy the relaxing and healing properties of essential oils before you drift to sleep.

CHAPTER 17

Dream Symbols and Metaphors

Dreams are the progressive story written from our soul.

Our dreams tell the story of our journey through life. Our psyche projects memories of the interactions we share with others and the places, sensations, traumas, smells, feelings, tastes, and thoughts we encounter throughout our lifetime. From these collective experiences, our psyche projects the details of these events into the dream realm, using specific metaphors, symbols, scenery, and themes.

If our goal is to learn, interpret, and be guided by our dreams, we need to ditch the habit of choosing one or two symbols from our dreams and focusing all our energy into deciphering what they mean. Our dreams should not be reduced or limited to a single interpretation of one symbol/metaphor because this causes us to lose sight of the collective story the dream is relaying. I prompt you to begin looking at your dream as you would a story that you are about to sit down and read. You would not just read one or two pages from a novel and try to grasp what the story is about. Instead, you would read all the words to fully appreciate and understand the story.

As you would have undoubtedly noticed throughout this book, I am opposed to turning to objective, preconceived 'online dream symbol interpretations' as I believe no one can interpret your dream more accurately and intuitively than you can. If your psyche, memories, and life experiences generate your dreams, then how can anyone besides you truly understand the story your soul is writing every time you fall asleep?

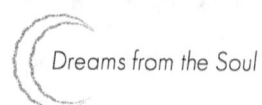
Dreams from the Soul

Self-reflection

To guide you with your dream work, I have created three simple questions for you to ask yourself upon awakening from a dream. These self-reflective questions will help you to connect deeply with your dreaming experience and invoke an intuitive ability to interpret dream metaphors and messages:

1) What thoughts and emotions are flowing through me regarding the dream I had?
2) Is the dream making me question anything?
3) Can I relate anything from the dream back to my life?

Answering these questions in your dream journal or during reflective meditation will help you to fully capture the essence of your dream experience.

1) Writing down the emotions and thoughts that are arising for you, and any themes/symbols from the dream that may be triggering you, helps your higher self connect with the dream in a powerful and meaningful way.

2) When you stop to reflect on your dream without the urgency to analyse it, you will notice that certain questions and interest will arise in your mind about particular life events, situations, decisions, and yourself. This reflective process allows for revelations, answers, guidance, clarity, and introspection to occur.

3) Connecting elements from your dream and relating them back to your life will assist you in beginning to recognise the recurring dream metaphors your collective consciousness uses. For example, you may notice you dream of raging fires when you are under great stress, or you dream of an aggressive werewolf when your partner drinks too much alcohol and scares you with their behaviour.

Below is a hypothetical example of how it would look to interpret a dream using this three-step questioning method.

Dream example

You dream of a wild crocodile at your workplace. It is walking around your boss's office where you need to enter, and blood is all over the floor.

1) What thoughts and emotions are arising for me about this dream?

    Answer: *I'm frightened of the crocodile because I've seen on television how quickly they can strike and take down their prey. I don't like this dream at all because I know I have to enter my boss's office and that I will most likely be attacked. I feel upset.*

2) Is the dream making me question anything?

    Answer: *If the dream had kept going, I don't know whether I would have walked into my boss's office. I wonder if I'd have had the courage to face the crocodile. Why didn't I think to find something to hit the crocodile with instead of just standing in the doorway scared?*

3) Can I relate anything from the dream back to my life?

    Answer: *The crocodile reminds me of my new boss, who is ruthless and volatile. He has been firing people from the company, including my good friend and colleague, who is extremely upset and scared for her financial situation. I worry that I'll lose my job soon and it's causing me a lot of anxiety because I don't know where I would go.*

Break down the metaphors from the dream and relate them back to real life:

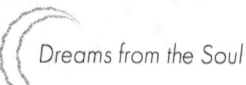

- Crocodile = ruthless and volatile work boss.
- Blood on the floor = people who have been fired, including good friend and work colleague.
- Standing in boss's doorway scared = uncertainty and anxiety about what to do if fired from job.

From solely answering the three questions and clarifying the main metaphors, we can see the hypothetical dreamer has quickly and accurately interpreted their dream. If you feel drawn to further reflect on your dream in the following days or weeks, you may unexpectedly notice a significant detail that suddenly stands out to you. For example, if we look at the answer to question two – *Why didn't I think to find something to hit the crocodile with instead of just standing in the doorway scared?* – the dreamer may suddenly realise that their 'hesitation' in the dream may be a wake-up call to start being more assertive. Instead of waiting around with anxiety and worry about the potential outcome of their job, it would be wiser to take the initiative and look for another one.

I hope after reading this example that you can see how limited it would have been if we tried to solely interpret the meaning of the 'crocodile and blood on the floor'. This is how we are most often told to interpret our dreams, but ultimately this ends up restricting us greatly and does not allow for spiritual, intuitive, and personal growth to occur.

Your dreams are your own. Explore them deeply with your higher self, imagination, feelings, and intuition.

Interpretation and understanding

We are now going to explore popular symbols and metaphors that frequently surface in the dream realm. Rather than providing you with a final interpretation of what they mean, I have listed prompting questions to ask yourself and possible meanings that coincide with the energy of the dream theme.

* **Arriving late/running behind – associated with:**
  - slowing down
  - being present
  - re-engagement with personal interests and passions
  - dormancy and stagnating
  - motivation
  - exhaustion
  - lost opportunities.

  Questions to ask yourself:

* What do I feel like I am missing out on?
* Am I just going through the motions every day, without truly enjoying myself?
* Have I been focusing enough on my ambitions, plans and interests, or have I been too preoccupied with life's responsibilities?
* Is there something in my life I could be developing or working towards?
* Are societal expectations controlling me?
* Do I have a healthy work and home balance?

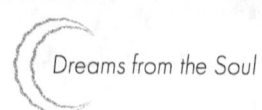

Key words: personal interests, rat-race, unacknowledged knowledge, tediousness, integrating simplicity, mindfulness, and balance into life schedule.

* **Asylum – associated with:**
    ☾ conflict
    ☾ resolution
    ☾ breakdown
    ☾ time out and space
    ☾ warning.

    Questions to ask yourself:

* Am I pushing myself to the extreme?
* What is causing me great stress right now? Do I have any control over it, or do I have to step back and allow things to unfold?
* Is my mental health in a good place?
* Are their toxic people in my life who carry more drama and problems, rather than happiness and love for me?
* What am I not expressing to myself or others?

Key words: mental health, challenges, setbacks, bad luck, negativity, self-care, introducing beneficial changes to wellbeing and health routines.

* **Attending a lecture/being in a classroom – associated with:**
    ☾ a lesson being passed on to you from the universe
    ☾ paying attention to advice that is offered to you or when information crosses your path
    ☾ learning from past mistakes

Dream Symbols and Metaphors

- ☾ turning to a mentor or trusted person for support, guidance, and help.

Questions to ask yourself:

* Do I need to reach out and ask for help?
* Am I dealing with a situation I have already dealt with in the past? If so, what did I learn and how can I apply it to my current circumstances?
* Am I being stubborn when I should be open-minded to what others have to say?

Key words: consideration, support, guidance, community.

* **Being lost – associated with:**
  - ☾ lack of direction
  - ☾ troubled mindset
  - ☾ self-imposed restrictions
  - ☾ instincts and intuition being ignored or disregarded
  - ☾ boredom of following the same monotonous routine
  - ☾ support systems.

Questions to ask yourself:

* Do I have any goals or plans for my future?
* Is my current routine becoming tedious?
* Am I being influenced by societal expectations instead of doing what I want to?
* Do I feel lost?

Key words: overlooking what is right in front of you, re-determining your vision, prioritisation, being open to advice, guidance, and help.

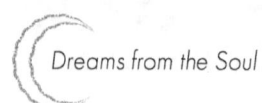
Dreams from the Soul

- **Car – associated with:**
  - (crash/accident) a warning to slow down; mentally, physically, emotionally, or materially, you are heading to breakdown and burnout
  - (driving) being in control of your life and deciding what is right for you in the present moment in time
  - (being a passenger) allowing others to dictate and influence your life, a lack of control, a need to step back and see things from a different perspective, accepting help from others (this symbol of being a 'passenger' has two different metaphorical meanings, so you will need to reflect closely on your life circumstances to determine how it relates to you).

Questions to ask yourself:

- Am I making the right decisions for both the immediate moment and future?
- Should I be looking at situations less emotionally and more objectively?
- Where is my life currently headed?
- Have I been taking control of my life or allowing others to control me?

Key words: personal space, routine, organisation, independence, choices.

- **Construction zone – associated with:**
  - additional time, care, and effort needing to be dedicated to a specific area of your life
  - taking new and positive approaches
  - self-improvement and looking after your wellbeing

- ☾ a reassessment of life's priorities.

Questions to ask yourself:

- ✲ Is there an area of my life I have been neglecting?
- ✲ What do I need to start doing less or more of?
- ✲ How can I rearrange my schedule to create more time to focus on…?

Key words: practicality, decluttering, nurture, restoring balance.

- ✲ **Devil – associated with:**
    - ☾ self-loathing
    - ☾ bullying, hostility, abuse
    - ☾ negative energy
    - ☾ toxic environments and people
    - ☾ danger and recklessness
    - ☾ desire, lust, and anger.

Questions to ask yourself:

- ✲ Am I letting others control me and dictate what I do?
- ✲ Do I let the opinions of others determine my sense of worth?
- ✲ Am I ignoring the warning signs my intuition is telling me?
- ✲ Have I been angry, easily triggered, impatient, and rude to others?
- ✲ Am I doing something I should not be? Am I crossing the line with something or someone?

Key words: turmoil energy, emotions, and mindset; manipulation, violence, potential risks, need to escape, temptation.

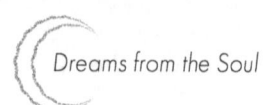

- **Dying/death – associated with:**
  - (if you see yourself dying in a dream) uncertainty, awaiting answers and guidance, self-reflection of life direction, changes, blocked chakras, being held back, problems from the past, conflicted mindset, unbalanced energy
  - (if you see yourself die in a dream) change, transition, revelation, self-awareness, new cycle, endings, transformation, spiritual awakening.

  Questions to ask yourself:

- Am I paying attention to the signs from my intuition and the universe?
- Is there something from my past holding me back?
- Do I have any regrets, unfinished business, or memories from the past I keep dwelling on?
- Who am I and what is my purpose right now?

Key words: health ailments, disharmony, stress, next chapter, releasing the old and welcoming the new.

- **Elevator – associated with:**
  - (travelling upwards) unconsciously trusting your intuition and the signs the universe is leaving you, feeling of being in control, clear intentions, and looking ahead not behind
  - (travelling downwards) approaching situations blindly, being reclusive, delays, unwelcome news, and wrong timing
  - (stuck in an elevator) an inability to be objective, truthful, and open about what you are feeling, thinking, and going through.

Questions to ask yourself:

* Where am I being guided at this time?
* Is there something I need to get off my chest to move forward with my life?
* Am I hiding from something?

Key words: overthinking, faith, communication.

* **Falling off a tree/tripping on a tree branch – associated with:**
    ☾ unexpected delays or momentary setbacks
    ☾ a need for caution
    ☾ a sudden uproot in plans, ideas, direction in life (especially in the sense of priorities).

Questions to ask yourself:

* Am I currently guiding myself in the right direction?
* What are my objectives in the present moment, and do they need to change?
* Am I being careful with my words and actions?

Key words: patience, self-awareness, change.

* **Fence – associated with:**
    ☾ (wooden fence) everyday life problems such as momentary stresses, challenges, and disagreements
    ☾ (wire fence) psychological isolation, repression, fear, doubt, and anxiety
    ☾ (raggedy old falling-down fence) the collapse of something in waking life; e.g., increasingly defeated and turmoil mindset, problems will not subside, feeling down on luck and overwhelmed

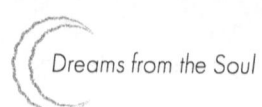

- ☾ (building a fence) creating new (healthy) boundaries in life, self-development, and emotional and physical strength
- ☾ (climbing or jumping a fence) self-confidence, overcoming limitations, and restrictions.

Questions to ask yourself:

* Can I work on changing my current circumstances? If this is not possible, can I react or approach things in a different manner?
* What is the biggest block or obstacle in my life right now?
* What am I overcoming or moving towards?

Key words: hurdles, problem-solving, focus, intention.

* **Flying – associated with:**
    - ☾ stepping out of comfort zone
    - ☾ freedom
    - ☾ liberation from the things that once held you back
    - ☾ individuality
    - ☾ independence
    - ☾ long-term decisions
    - ☾ escape.

Questions to ask yourself:

* Am I floating through life aimlessly or do I know where I am heading?
* When was the last time I had a holiday and escaped the daily routine?
* Am I at a point in my life where I no longer need people or items to make me happy?

- ✳ How do I determine my sense of happiness, abundance, and freedom?
- ✳ Am I excessive with anything? Do I need to de-clutter my life?

Key words: cleaning, simplicity, personal growth, shifting priorities, movement, new direction, relaxation, balanced chakras, healing.

- ✳ **Giving birth/baby – associated with:**
  - ☾ a new chapter in life journey
  - ☾ positive universal energy heading to you
  - ☾ creation and manifestation
  - ☾ receiving recognition for something you do
  - ☾ discovering a new interest or creative outlet.

Questions to ask yourself:

- ✳ Do I trust the universe and what it has in store for me?
- ✳ Am I ready to explore the world more deeply?
- ✳ Have I been dedicating enough time to my dreams?
- ✳ Have I asked my spirit guides for help in finding my next path?

Key words: opportunity, personal potential, nurturing relationships with others and oneself, optimism.

- ✳ **Key – associated with:**
  - ☾ intuitive knowledge
  - ☾ taking initiative
  - ☾ trusting your instincts and making logical decisions
  - ☾ information
  - ☾ possibilities.

Questions to ask yourself:

* Am I hesitating about doing something?
* Do I worry too much about what 'could potentially' happen, instead of just taking a calculated risk?
* When was the last time I turned to my higher self for answers?

Key words: trusting the process, even when the outcome is unknown, resourcefulness, guidance, being open-minded to new experiences and ways of being.

* **Ladder – associated with:**
  * (climbing a ladder) striving for goals, manifesting abundance, and stepping out of your comfort zone
  * (going down a ladder) a need for retreat and redirection of energy and focus
  * (stuck on a ladder) making little to no progress with plans and goals
  * (falling off a ladder) sudden disruption appearing in life
  * (steps missing from a ladder/wobbly ladder) the path will not be easy, and issues will surface along the way.

Questions to ask yourself:

* Have I been making progress and sticking to my goals?
* What lessons have I learnt so far from this experience?
* Am I making things harder for myself than they truly need to be?

Key words: ambition, motivation, persistence.

Dream Symbols and Metaphors

- **Looking at paintings/being in an art gallery – associated with:**
  - perspective
  - introspection
  - psyche
  - emerging ideas, philosophical views, and self-examination
  - creativity and artistry
  - personal growth
  - deeper understanding of other viewpoints and belief systems
  - conversation/socialising.

Questions to ask yourself:

- Am I being guided to new beliefs, pathways, and people?
- Do I appreciate and value diversity?
- Do I understand that everyone is different, including myself, and this is a wonderful thing?
- Is it time for me to embrace a new creative or ambitious outlet?
- When was the last time I meditated, connected with my higher self, talked with my guides, and manifested my dreams to the universe?

Key words: travel, connection, adventure, life lessons, acceptance, respect, tapping into existing or newfound skills.

- **Motorbike – associated with:**
  - ego, passion, and spontaneity
  - recklessness and carefree attitude

- ☾ impatience and arrogance
- ☾ freedom.

Questions to ask yourself:

- ✳ Am I pushing the boundaries a little too far?
- ✳ Will my current choices and actions have possible consequences down the track?
- ✳ How have I been behaving and organising my life lately?
- ✳ Is it time to start having more fun?

Key words: impulsive choices, courage, self-expression.

✳ **Nudity/lack of clothing – associated with:**
- ☾ vulnerability
- ☾ insecurity
- ☾ nervousness, doubts, anxiety, and uncertainty
- ☾ opening-up, self-expression, and honesty
- ☾ losing sight of what is important.

Questions to ask yourself:

- ✳ Am I showing the 'real' me to everyone, or am I hiding behind a façade?
- ✳ What is currently worrying or weighing down on me?
- ✳ How do I see myself and how do I think others see me?
- ✳ What am I holding myself back from?
- ✳ What do I need to let go of or stop doing to find happiness?

Key words: inhibition, disclosure, hesitation, self-doubt, contemplation, authenticity.

- **Paparazzi surrounding you – associated with:**
  - (enjoying being in the spotlight) socialising, attending gatherings with family and friends, self-confidence, healthy ego, enjoyment, recognition, self-expression, and enjoyment
  - (not enjoying being in the spotlight) unhappiness, insecurity, embarrassment, focusing too closely on what you consider to be your flaws, gossiping, and feeling that you do not fit in.

  Questions to ask yourself:
- Am I happy with myself?
- How can I share my positivity, talent, and skills with others?
- Am I being too hard on myself and comparing what I look like to others?
- Is it time to start spending time with new people?

Key words: celebration, self-expression, low self-esteem, self-love.

- **Parking lot – associated with:**
  - discombobulated thought patterns
  - needing to re-evaluate your next move or decision
  - dedicating time out to 'pause' from life, stressors, and problems.

  Questions to ask yourself:
- Have I looked at all my options?
- Do I need to shift my current train of thought to see things in a different light?
- Have I turned within and listened to what my instincts are guiding me to do?

Dreams from the Soul

* Am I constantly on the go and neglecting my personal needs?

Key words: intuition, knowledge, problem-solving.

* **Plane – associated with:**
    ☾ (flying in a plane) a desire to travel, excitement, life choices, independence, and positive omen for possibilities and future opportunities
    ☾ (plane crash) situations not going according to plan, lacking creativity and enthusiasm, pessimism, fear, depressing outlook on life, and unforeseen setbacks
    ☾ (missing your flight) a lost opportunity, ignoring aspirations and goals, inadequate self-care, indecision, lack of direction, and anxiety.

Questions to ask yourself:

* Are there any opportunities or ideas I want to pursue?
* Am I looking at life with a negative mindset?
* Is it time for a change of some kind?
* Have I been putting myself first or others?

Key words: adventure, manifestation, independence, unexpected news, acceptance, movement.

* **Pregnancy – associated with:**
    ☾ creativity and new ideas
    ☾ spiritual, personal, or material growth
    ☾ change
    ☾ adapting to new circumstances and introducing new ways of doing old things
    ☾ new beginnings

Dream Symbols and Metaphors

☾ the early stages of something developing – this may not be consciously recognised yet.

Questions to ask yourself:

❋ Is it time for something new to begin in my life?
❋ Have I been contemplating something?
❋ Do I have faith in myself to bring my ideas, dreams, and goals to life?
❋ Am I nurturing myself and others?

Key words: blessings, self-awareness, intuitive messages, expansion, transformation.

❋ **Railroad/train tracks – associated with:**

☾ (crossing railroad tracks) stepping into a new phase of your journey, ending and new beginnings, and releasing unnecessary burden
☾ (falling on a railroad track) divine intervention, the inevitable will occur, an omen of change
☾ (building a railroad track) sparked ideas, and the early stages of something new forming in your mind or life, such as pursuing a new interest, creative outlet, or job.

Questions to ask yourself:

❋ Am I ready to experience something new in my life?
❋ What do I need to let go of that is ultimately holding me back?
❋ If change occurs, will I be accepting or closed off from it?
❋ Am I trusting my intuition and where it is guiding me?

Key words: acknowledging thought patterns, taking calculated risks, embracing the future.

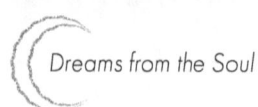

✷ Staircase – associated with:

- ☾ (spiral staircase) slower-moving progress, the workings of destiny, patience, hidden knowledge

  Message: do not expect everything to happen at once. The path you seek, the goals you aspire to reach, and the people you are meant to meet will come into your life when the time is right.

- ☾ (narrow staircase) simplicity, effective time management, stress, overworking, restriction, a shift in perspective, stubbornness, being open to alternative options

  Message: be mindful with how you direct your thoughts and energy. Do not shut people out of your life or lose sight of what truly matters to you.

- ☾ (wide staircase) growth, expansion, multiple choices, ideas

  Message: the sky is the limit when it comes to what you do next in your life. Go out into the world and discover new things, do not hold yourself back.

- ☾ (falling down a staircase) minor accidents, mistakes, mental blocks, setbacks, disagreements, a need for time out

  Message: you cannot control the annoying disruptions, stagnancy, or bad luck you seem to be experiencing lately. So, take a step back from it all and let yourself relax.

Questions to ask yourself:

✷ How am I using my time, energy, resources, and personal potential?

- ✺ Am I following the same path constantly? Is it time for a change, to try new approaches to old problems, or introduce spontaneity into my daily routine?
- ✺ Why am I currently doing the things I do? Have I gotten stuck in a cycle that is no longer fulfilling to me?
- ✺ What is holding me back or what do I 'feel' is holding me back right now?

Key words: discovery, realisations, limitations, motivation, and choices.

- ✺ **Teeth falling out/rotten or decaying teeth – associated with:**
    - ☾ stress
    - ☾ anxiety, worry, and panic
    - ☾ mental exhaustion
    - ☾ lost or unacknowledged opportunities
    - ☾ feeling left behind or lacking in some type of way compared to others
    - ☾ self-criticism.

    Questions to ask yourself:
- ✺ Have I had a lot on my plate lately?
- ✺ What thoughts keep running through my mind, and why?
- ✺ What can I do to increase my happiness?
- ✺ Have I been closing myself off from positive experiences, fun, and pleasure?

Key words: disinterest, self-worth, tiredness, lack of motivation, inspiration.

Your Journey

I hope you found inspiration and guidance within the pages of this book. My wish is for more people to connect with their higher self, dreams, and the spirit world because your life journey and destiny are so deeply influenced by these elements. Never doubt your ability to understand and intuitively interpret your dreams. Ultimately, they are a manifestation of your spirit, soul, collective consciousness, past lives, and authenticity.

In the beautiful, poetic words of DH LAWRENCE:

All people dream, but not equally.
Those who dream by night in the dusty recesses of their mind,
wake in the morning to find that it was vanity.
But the dreamers of the day are dangerous people,
for they dream their dreams with open eyes,
and make them come true.

About the Author

Taylar Brooker has a strong connection to the dream and spirit world. She has been a professional tarot reader (Tarot Taylar) for the past four years and has read for over 700 clients. Following the profound dream visions of her Serpent Spirit Guide, the experience opened her eyes to the universal power, magick and wisdom that dreams possess.

As an emerging psychotherapist, Taylar aspires to integrate dream work and interpretation, intuitive journaling, spirituality, and eco-psychology in her future therapeutic practice. When she is not working or studying, Taylar enjoys collecting second-hand books, drinking copious amounts of tea, spending time in nature, and relaxing with her dogs.

Social media handles:

* Tarot Taylar – Facebook, Instagram, Tiktok
* Moonstone Mystic Au – Facebook, Instagram
* Website – MoonstoneGypsyAU.com